Shortcuts for
easy homemade cooking

My Secret Cookbook

by Paula Simmons

Author of
THE ZUCCHINI COOKBOOK

Try
my
Secrets!
Paula

Pacific Search Press

Pacific Search Press, 222 Dexter Avenue North,
     Seattle, Washington 98109
©1979 by Paula Simmons. All rights reserved
Printed in the United States of America

Edited by Miriam Remak Bulmer
Designed by Paula Schlosser
Block print on cover by Diana L. Fairbanks

Library of Congress Cataloging in Publication Data

Simmons, Paula.
    My secret cookbook.
    Includes index.
    1. Cookery.   I. Title.
TX715.S598   641.5   79-4181
ISBN 0-914718-43-6

Contents

Cooking— The Smart and Lazy Way

My husband calls me smart and lazy. I don't like to go to much bother about cooking, so I'm always coming up with ways to make things easier or faster or to bamboozle my husband and friends into thinking I've done a lot of work. Cooking is a lot more interesting and more enjoyable if I think I'm outwitting the system, doing something I'm not supposed to be doing.

Some of the recipes in this cookbook were developed when I worked part time. I wanted to come home and get dinner on the table with a minimum of preparation time, using things that were already partially prepared. Because I make mixes in large quantities before I need them, and because I always have canned fruit on the shelf, I've really taken the fuss out of cooking. I guess I spend about twenty minutes each night cooking dinner—and that can include a pie for dessert!

Other recipes (and my two other cookbooks, *The Zucchini Cookbook* and *The Green Tomato Cookbook*) have evolved out of a good garden. I like to raise things that grow fast and are easy to take care of—zucchinis and green tomatoes, for example. But many plants like that are also extremely prolific. Since my theory has always been "use what you have plenty of and use it in an imaginative way so that you don't get tired of the same doggone thing every night," I had to come up with a lot of recipes. That's a challenge many gardeners face come harvest time.

I'm also fortunate to have friends who share recipes with me. Quite often one of them will hand me a recipe saying, "You like to do things the easy way. Just wait until you try this!" A nice gift that one friend can give to another is an easy way to do something. This cookbook may not make you a smarter or lazier cook, but it will give you some shortcuts. I hope you—and your friends—will enjoy every minute of the time you will save using these recipes.

Homemade Mixes, Ready-Mades, and Seasonings

This section is made up of items you can prepare ahead in large quantities in order to save time later. You'll find they save quite a bit of money, too, and you are assured of having food that is free of artificial flavorings, colorings, and preservatives.

Most of the recipes are for dry mixes you can store in canisters. Store-bought mixes are always premeasured, but when you make your own, you can dip out whatever amount you really prefer to make.

My piecrust mix is a good example of the virtues of homemade mixes. It probably doesn't take five minutes more to make a big batch of mix than it does to make a single piecrust. (I figure it takes the same amount of time to get out the ingredients for ten piecrusts as it does for one.) I've always got some on hand, so when friends invite me over, I can say, "I'll make a couple of pies and bring them over in an hour." They think I can't do it, but I just open the canister, take out a cup of mix, roll it out, and there's my piecrust. I take some canned fruit off the shelf, fill the shell, spread some topping mix over the fruit, and it's ready to bake. No big deal.

Instant Hot Cocoa Mix

Most cocoa mixes need to be added to milk. This one has powdered milk right in it. It's a good mix to use at home, or you can package it in premeasured amounts and use it on camping trips.

Nonfat dry milk   3 cups
Unsweetened cocoa   ½ cup
Sugar   1 cup
Salt   a pinch
Plain malted milk powder   ½ cup (optional)

Combine all ingredients; store in airtight container. Makes about 5 cups of mix. To serve, place 2 tablespoons in a large mug, add ⅓ cup hot water, and stir until smooth. Add enough boiling water to fill mug and stir again.

Fireside Coffee Mix

The nondairy creamer makes this very rich. It's a Swiss Mocha-type coffee—a fun thing for winter.

Instant Hot Cocoa Mix   2 cups
Instant coffee powder   1 cup
Nondairy creamer   2 cups
Sugar   1½ cups
Cinnamon   ½ teaspoon
Nutmeg   ¼ teaspoon

In large bowl, blend cocoa, coffee, and powdered creamer with electric mixer for several minutes, then stir in sugar and spices. Store in tightly covered container at cool temperature. Makes 7 cups of mix. To serve, add 3 to 4 heaping teaspoons to a large cup of boiling water.

Pancake Mix

This is a very flexible recipe. You can use any combination of flours—whatever you happen to have on hand.

Unbleached flour 3 cups unsifted
Whole wheat flour 2 cups
Sugar ¼ cup
Powdered milk 1½ cups
Baking powder ¼ cup
Salt 1 tablespoon

Mix ingredients thoroughly. Store in tightly covered container, such as a ½-gallon canning jar, at cool temperature. Makes about 7 cups of mix.

Pancakes

Pancake Mix 1½ cups
Egg 1
Cold water ¾ cup
Margarine 2 tablespoons, melted

Combine all ingredients, stirring only until mixed. Spoon onto hot greased griddle and cook until browned on both sides, turning once. Makes 2 generous servings.

Orange-Date Pancakes

Pancake batter
Dates to taste, chopped
Orange peel to taste, grated
Honey 1 cup
Concentrated frozen orange juice 3 tablespoons
Margarine 1 tablespoon

Make pancake batter as directed in Pancakes recipe. Add dates and orange peel to pancake batter; cook on hot greased griddle until browned on both sides. Heat remaining ingredients together and serve as syrup.

Clafouti

This is a good way to use leftover batter.

Apples, peaches, cherries, or other fruit   unsweetened
Pancake batter (see Index)   to cover fruit
Sugar   to taste
Cream, whipped cream, ice cream, or liqueur   topping

Arrange fruit in greased flan pan; cover with pancake batter, sprinkle with sugar, and bake at 400° for 20 to 30 minutes, or until done. Serve with cream.

Biscuit Mix

Unbleached flour   8 cups or
    Unbleached flour and fine whole wheat flour   8 cups
Baking powder   6 tablespoons
Powdered milk   1½ cups
Salt   1 tablespoon
Margarine   1 cup

Mix together dry ingredients, then cut in margarine with pastry blender or mix with electric mixer at low speed until mixture forms very fine crumbs. Place in airtight container. Store in cool place; refrigerate during warm weather. Makes about ½ gallon of mix. To make biscuits, measure any amount of dry mixture into bowl and add just enough cold water to form a soft dough. Turn out onto floured surface; knead lightly. Roll to ½-inch thickness and cut into biscuits. Bake at 425° for 10 minutes, or until lightly browned.
Variations: Stir in sage and poultry seasoning before adding liquid, to make biscuits to accompany chicken or turkey. Mix in shredded cheese to make cheese biscuits.

Cornmeal Mix

Cornmeal 6 cups
Flour 5 cups unsifted
Sugar ⅔ cup
Baking powder ½ cup
Salt 5 teaspoons
Margarine 1⅓ cups

Combine all dry ingredients; mix well. Cut in margarine with pastry blender until mixture is crumbly. Store in covered container at cool temperature. Makes about 1 gallon of mix.

Cornbread

Cornmeal Mix 2½ cups
Egg 1
Milk 1 cup

Beat ingredients together until smooth. Pour into oiled 8 by 8-inch pan and bake 20 to 25 minutes at 425°.
Variation: Pour cornbread batter into hot greased corn-stick pans. Bake 20 to 25 minutes at 425°. Makes 12 to 14 corn sticks.

Cornmeal Muffins

Egg 1
Milk 1¼ cups
Cornmeal Mix 3 cups

Mix egg and milk together, then stir into Cornmeal Mix, stirring only until mixed. Fill well-greased muffin tins ⅔ full. Bake 12 to 15 minutes at 425°. Makes 12 medium muffins.

Cornmeal Pancakes

Cornmeal Mix (see Index)   3 cups
Eggs   2
Milk or skim milk   1¾ cups

Mix ingredients together, leaving batter a bit lumpy. Drop by large spoonfuls onto lightly greased hot griddle. When tops are bubbly, turn and brown other side. Serves 4.
Variation: Use this batter in your waffle iron to make Cornmeal Waffles.

Refrigerator Bran Muffins

This is actually a batter. When you want muffins, you just dip into it and fill as many little muffin tins as you want.

Margarine   1 cup, melted and cooled or
    Oil   1 cup
Sugar   2 cups
Eggs   4
Sour milk* or buttermilk   1 quart
Salt   2 teaspoons
Baking soda   2 tablespoons
40% Bran Flakes   1 15-ounce package
Flour   5 cups
Raisins, chopped nuts, or chopped dates   1 cup (optional)

In large bowl, beat margarine and sugar into eggs, then beat in sour milk. Beat in salt and soda, stir in bran flakes, then add flour; blend well. Stir in raisins. This batter will keep up to 6 weeks if stored in tightly covered container in the refrigerator. Makes 2½ to 3 quarts of batter. To bake muffins, fill greased muffin cups ⅔ full. Bake at 400° for about 15 minutes.
* To make sour milk, stir 2 tablespoons of lemon juice into 1 quart of milk; set aside 5 minutes before using.

Brown-and-Serve Rolls

When I bake bread, I nearly always put some aside as rolls. If you've got the oven hot anyway, then you can take these out of the refrigerator, pop them in, and you've got fresh-baked rolls for supper.

Homemade Bread dough (see Index)
Oil   for dipping

Shape dough into dinner rolls, about the size of golf balls or smaller. Dip each in oil and place in small, buttered foil pans or in 8 by 8-inch baking pan; use 9 to 12 per pan. Let rolls rise to nearly double. Bake at 275° for 30 minutes, then remove from oven. Leave rolls in pans and cool on rack for 10 minutes, then remove from pans and place on racks until completely cooled. Seal cooled rolls in plastic bag; they will keep in the refrigerator for up to 2 weeks. You can also double-wrap and freeze them. To serve, bake rolls at 450° for 5 minutes, or until brown. Bake frozen rolls for 10 minutes.

Campfire Bread Mix

I'm not a camper; I'm a friend of a camper.

Unbleached flour   3 cups unsifted
Fine whole wheat flour   3 cups
Salt   2 teaspoons
Powdered milk   1 cup
Baking powder   ¼ cup
Margarine   1 cup
Rolled oats   1 cup
Wheat germ   1 cup

Mix together first 5 ingredients. Cut in margarine with pastry blender until mixture forms fine crumbs, then stir in oats and wheat germ. Store covered in cool place or in refrigerator. For camping, measure out desired quantities for each meal and seal in plastic bags. Makes about ½ gallon of mix. To make Campfire Bread, mix any amount of dry mix with just enough cold water to make firm dough. Pat out to ½-inch thickness on cornmealed surface, and cut into squares, circles, or wedges. Dip tops and cut edges in leftover cornmeal. Fry slowly in skillet, browning both sides. These also cook well in a reflector oven or in a Dutch oven buried in hot coals.

Vegetable Cream Sauce Mix

I always keep a quart jar of this mix in the refrigerator during fresh vegetable season. We often eat the same vegetable three or four days in a row when the garden is producing at its best; sometimes we get an overabundance of one vegetable for a few weeks. Using the mix, plus one of the variations, can make a vegetable taste different each night.

All-purpose flour   ½ cup unsifted
Powdered skim milk   ½ cup
Onion powder   2 teaspoons
Seasoning salt   ½ teaspoon
Salt   1 teaspoon
Freshly ground pepper   ½ teaspoon
Margarine   ½ cup

Mix dry ingredients, then cut in margarine with a pastry blender or with an electric mixer on low speed, until mixture forms fine crumbs. Store in tightly covered jar in refrigerator. Makes about 1 cup of mix. To make Cream Sauce, boil vegetables, then drain off and measure your cooking liquid. Add 2 heaping tablespoons of mix to ½ cup of hot vegetable liquid, or 5 tablespoons to 1 cup of liquid. Return mixture to heat and boil 3 minutes, beating with a whisk. Add drained vegetables, reheat, and serve.

Variations: You may add shredded cheese, curry powder, powdered horseradish, mustard, or special herbs to vary the sauce and to suit the vegetable you are serving.

Oven-Baked Chicken Coating Mix

This has kind of a barbecued taste.

Flour ¼ cup
Fine dry bread crumbs 2 cups
Salt 4 teaspoons
Sugar 2 teaspoons
Garlic powder ½ teaspoon
Onion powder 2 teaspoons
Paprika 3 tablespoons
Ground oregano 2 teaspoons
Cayenne ½ teaspoon or less
Margarine ¼ cup

Mix together dry ingredients. Cut in margarine with pastry blender or with electric mixer on low speed, until mixture is crumbly. Store in tightly covered container in a cool place. Makes about 2⅔ cups of mix. To use, dip chicken pieces in milk, skim milk, or buttermilk, then dip them in mix. For a crispier coating, allow pieces to dry 1 hour before baking. Bake at 375° to 400° for 45 minutes, or until chicken is tender. If it gets too brown before it is done, cover loosely with foil.

Cornstarch Pudding Mix

When you buy pudding mixes in the store, you're paying umpteen times the price of the ingredients. This one is much cheaper, you can measure it out in smaller quantities, and it keeps almost indefinitely.

Powdered milk 4 cups
Cornstarch 1½ cups
Sugar 2 cups
Salt 1½ teaspoons

Mix ingredients well. Store in tightly covered canister or ½-gallon jar; keep in cool place. Makes about 7½ cups of mix.

Basic Pudding

Cold water   1 cup
Cornstarch Pudding Mix (see Index)   1⅛ cups
Boiling water   1 cup
Margarine   2 tablespoons, or less
Vanilla   1 teaspoon

Mix cold water with Cornstarch Pudding Mix in saucepan. Add boiling water and mix well. Bring to a boil, stirring constantly. Boil 3 minutes, then stir in margarine and vanilla; remove from heat. Cool 15 minutes, stirring occasionally. Spoon into glasses and chill. Serves 4.
Variations: Layer pudding and fruit in parfait glasses. To use as pie filling, use 1⅔ cups liquid instead of 2 cups. Cool 15 minutes, stir well, and turn into baked pie shell; chill well. Garnish with fruit or whipped cream.

Chocolate Pudding

Cocoa   1 tablespoon
Sugar   1 tablespoon
Cornstarch Pudding Mix (see Index)

Stir cocoa and sugar into pudding mix as it is measured out, then follow Basic Pudding recipe.

Coconut Pudding

Basic Pudding
Coconut extract   ½ teaspoon
Shredded coconut   ½ cup

After Basic Pudding has boiled 3 minutes, add coconut extract and shredded coconut.

Festive Mocha Pudding

Cocoa   1 tablespoon
Cornstarch Pudding Mix (see Index)
Homemade Coffee Liqueur (see Index)   ½ cup

Stir cocoa into pudding mix as it is measured out, then follow Basic Pudding recipe, but use 1½ cups of water instead of 2. Remove pudding from heat after boiling 3 minutes, then stir in Homemade Coffee Liqueur along with margarine. Pour into parfait glasses and chill.

Basic Cookie Mix

Unbleached flour   2½ cups
Fine whole wheat flour   2 cups
Sugar   2¾ to 3 cups
Baking powder   3 tablespoons
Salt   1½ teaspoons
Margarine   2 cups, sliced
Rolled oats   8 cups

Mix together first 5 ingredients. Add margarine slices and cut in with pastry blender. Stir in oats. Store mixture in tightly covered container in cool place. Makes about 5 big batches of cookies.

Basic Sugar Cookies

Basic Cookie Mix   4 cups
Cinnamon   ½ teaspoon
Vanilla   1 teaspoon
Egg   1
Milk   3 tablespoons
Sugar   to coat cookies

Mix together all ingredients, then form into small balls, about 1 teaspoon each. Roll balls in sugar, place on oiled cookie sheet, and flatten. Bake at 350° for about 12 minutes, or until lightly browned. Makes 3 to 4 dozen cookies.
Variations: Add ½ cup of any of the following: chocolate chips, chopped nuts, raisins, chopped dates, or candied or dried fruit. To make coconut cookies, add 2 tablespoons of fine cookie coconut; roll balls in coconut before baking.

Refrigerator Oat Cookies

Drop cookies aren't much fun. If you don't make a big recipe, then you've spent all that time and you have only two dozen cookies to show for it. With a great big batch, it takes forever timing them—twelve minutes in the oven, take them out, put another batch in. The nice thing about Refrigerator Oat Cookies is that if you've heated up the oven for anything, you can open up the refrigerator, spoon them out on a cookie sheet, and push them in the oven. Pretty soon, the house smells like fresh cookies, everybody's happy, and—oh boy—you haven't done any work at all!

Margarine   2 cups
Brown sugar   2 cups, or to taste
Sugar   1 cup
Vanilla   2 teaspoons
Eggs   4
Flour   3 cups unsifted
Salt   1½ teaspoons
Baking soda   1 tablespoon
Rolled oats   6 cups
Nuts   1½ cups chopped or
    Shredded coconut   1½ cups

Beat together margarine and sugars until light and fluffy. Beat in vanilla and eggs. Stir together flour, salt, and baking soda; mix into creamed mixture. Stir in oats and nuts. Dough can now be stored in tightly covered container in the refrigerator for up to 2 weeks. Makes about 3 quarts of dough. To bake, drop by teaspoonfuls, 2 inches apart, on greased or nonstick cookie sheet. Bake at 350° for 10 to 14 minutes.
Variations: Substitute raisins or chopped dates for nuts or coconut.

Brownie Mix

Unbleached flour   3 cups
Fine whole wheat flour   3 cups
Sugar   7 cups
Cocoa   2½ cups
Salt   1 tablespoon
Baking powder   2 tablespoons
Margarine   2 cups

Mix dry ingredients well, using low speed of mixer. Cut in margarine until mixture is in fine crumbs. Store in tightly covered container in cool place. Makes about 3½ quarts of mix.

Brownies

Sprinkling the nuts on top of these brownies gives more nut taste with fewer nuts.

Brownie Mix   2 cups
Eggs   2
Vanilla   1½ teaspoons
Flour or cocoa   to dust pan
Nuts   chopped

Mix together Brownie Mix, eggs, and vanilla. Grease an 8 by 8-inch pan; dust with flour. Pour batter into pan and sprinkle with nuts. Bake at 350° for 20 to 25 minutes. Cool on wire rack; cut into squares.
Variation: To make mocha brownies, stir 1 tablespoon instant powdered coffee into mix before adding eggs and vanilla.

Fudge Brownie Pie

Brownies batter
Pie shell   9-inch, unbaked
Chocolate syrup   ¼ cup

Prepare batter according to Brownies recipe. Pour batter into pie shell; cover with chocolate syrup. Bake at 350° for about 40 minutes.

Brownie Pudding-Cake

Brownies batter (see Index)
Brown sugar   ⅔ cup
Cocoa   ¼ cup
Hot water   1½ cups

Prepare batter according to Brownies recipe. Pour into 9 by 9-inch pan. Mix together brown sugar and cocoa; sprinkle over batter. Carefully pour hot water over all. Bake at 350° for 45 minutes, or until cake parts are done. Serve warm.

Standard Piecrust Mix

Ordinarily, when I make piecrust, I use a little more water than most people because I find that the scraps are then much easier to reroll. I just flour my pastry cloth real well.

Flour   6 cups unsifted or
  Flour   3 cups unsifted and
  Whole wheat pastry flour   3 cups unsifted
Salt   2 teaspoons
Sugar   3 tablespoons
Noninstant powdered milk   ½ cup
Margarine   2 cups

Mix together dry ingredients. Cut in margarine with pastry blender until mixture forms fine crumbs. Store in tightly covered container in refrigerator or cool place. Makes about 1½ quarts of mix. To make piecrust, measure about 1½ cups mix for double crust 8-inch pie, and add enough cold water to make soft dough. Roll out, ½ at a time, on heavily floured pastry cloth, for each crust. Bake as usual, depending on type of filling used. For a baked pie shell, bake crust at 350° for 15 minutes, or until pale, golden brown.
Note: For fruit pies, brush the bottom crust with melted margarine before filling. For pumpkin pie, wipe out egg shells of eggs used in filling and brush on bottom crust before filling. This helps prevent a soggy crust.

Special Dry Piecrust Mix

If you want to make a cheesecake or use a pudding or a thickened fruit filling, this is a little richer crust than the rolled out crust. It's also fast! You just pat out as much as you need on the bottom of the pan—no need to add any liquid, and you won't have to get out the pastry cloth and get flour all over everything. Then you can either fill it and bake it, or bake it and then fill it, which is even better.

Unbleached flour   5 cups unsifted
Salt   1 teaspoon
Sugar   ¾ cup
Margarine   2 cups

Mix flour, salt, and sugar. Cut in margarine with pastry blender until mixture forms fine crumbs. Store in tightly covered jar in the refrigerator. Makes about 1½ quarts of mix. To make crust, stir mix, then measure. Press 1 cup of mix into bottom of an 8 by 8-inch or 9 by 9-inch baking pan; use 1½ cups of mix for 8-inch pie tin. Fill and bake as usual, depending on filling.
Variation: For a baked pie shell, bake crust at 350° for 12 to 15 minutes, or until pale, golden brown. Cool, then fill with cream or gelatin filling. A spoonful of the mix may be sprinkled around the edges on top to garnish cream pies.

Crumbly Dutch Topping Mix

If you use this as a topping on a fruit pie, the only work you have to do is roll out the piecrust mix. Cobblers are even easier. If it's fresh fruit, you don't even have to sweeten the fruit—just put the topping on it. It bakes into a nice, crusty, rich, sweet-tasting dish—with no work at all.

Sugar 2 cups
Flour 2 cups
Cinnamon 1 teaspoon
Nutmeg 1 teaspoon
Salt ¼ teaspoon
Margarine 1 cup

Mix together dry ingredients; cut in margarine with pastry blender. Store in airtight container and keep it cool. Makes about 1 quart of mix. To use on fruit pies, spread about ¾ cup of mix over canned or fresh fruit in an unbaked pie shell. Bake as usual, covering piecrust edge with a strip of foil to keep it from getting too brown. To use on individual cobblers, spread about ¼ cup of mix over unsweetened fresh fruit or drained home-canned fruit that has been arranged in individual ovenproof dishes. (Buttering the dish will make a richer cobbler.) Bake for 18 to 25 minutes at 375° to 400°, depending on whether you are baking it with other foods being prepared for supper. Topping should be nicely browned and fruit should be bubbly.

Note: This topping is best when served slightly warm, as it becomes less crisp when it sits around too long. You can recrisp it by placing it under the broiler, but watch carefully to prevent burning.

Plain Cake Mix

Cornstarch 1-pound package
Unbleached flour 5 pounds
Sugar 16 cups (about 8 pounds)
Baking powder ⅔ cup
Salt 1 heaping tablespoon
Margarine 3 pounds, sliced

In large canning kettle, mix all dry ingredients well; use electric mixer at low speed and alternate with mixing by hand, lifting the dry mixture up and turning it over. With medium speed of mixer, work in margarine until mixture is crumbly. Store in tightly covered canisters in cool, dry place. Spoon mixture into measuring cup when measuring. Makes about 1½ gallons of mix.

Plain Cake

Milk ¾ cup, lukewarm
Plain Cake Mix 3⅓ cups
Vanilla 1 teaspoon
Eggs 2

Add ½ the milk to mix and beat; add remaining milk. Add vanilla and eggs; beat 3 or 4 minutes, then pour into 2 greased and floured round cake pans, or one 9 by 13-inch baking pan. Bake at 350°; 25 minutes for layer pans, 30 to 40 minutes for larger pan.
Variation: Pour into cupcake tins and bake 10 to 15 minutes, or until done.

Spice Cake

Plain Cake ingredients
Cinnamon 1 teaspoon
Pumpkin pie spice 1 teaspoon
Raisins to taste (optional)
Nuts to taste (optional)

Use Plain Cake recipe, but add spices to dry mix before adding milk. Add raisins and nuts last.

Chocolate Cake

Plain Cake ingredients (see Index)
Cocoa   3 tablespoons
Cinnamon   ½ teaspoon
Nutmeg   ½ teaspoon

Use Plain Cake recipe, but add above ingredients to dry mix before adding milk.

Pineapple Cake

Plain Cake ingredients (see Index)
Pineapple juice   ⅔ cup
Pineapple flavoring   1 teaspoon
Crushed pineapple   ½ cup well drained

Use Plain Cake recipe, but substitute pineapple juice for milk and pineapple flavoring for vanilla. Fold pineapple into batter before pouring into pans.

Coconut Cake

Plain Cake ingredients (see Index)
Shredded coconut   1 cup
Low-Sugar Filling (see Index)

Use Plain Cake recipe, but sprinkle ½ cup coconut over each layer before baking. After baking, turn layers out of pans and cool on rack, coconut side up. Place bottom layer coconut side down, spread with Low-Sugar Filling, and cover with top layer, coconut side up.

Orange Cake

Plain Cake ingredients
Orange juice   ¾ cup
Orange extract   ½ teaspoon
Sugar   ¼ cup
Fresh orange peel   1 teaspoon, grated or
   Powdered orange peel   1 teaspoon

Use Plain Cake recipe, but substitute orange juice for milk, and use orange extract instead of vanilla. Mix sugar and orange peel; sprinkle over cake before baking.
Variation: Omit sugar and orange peel topping. Bake cake; top while hot with glaze made from ½ cup powdered sugar and ¼ cup orange juice.

Upside-Down Cake

Margarine   ½ cup
Brown sugar   1¾ cups
Fresh apples, cherries, or other fruit   to taste or
   Canned fruit (any kind)   to taste, well drained
Plain Cake batter (see Index)
Whipping cream   topping, whipped

Melt margarine in 9 by 13-inch pan; spread with brown sugar. Arrange fruit over sugar. Mix cake batter according to Plain Cake recipe, then pour over fruit. Bake at 350° for 30 to 40 minutes. Cool in pan, then turn upside down. Serve with whipped cream.

Gingerbread Mix

Flour   8 cups unsifted or
     Flour and whole wheat pastry flour   8 cups unsifted
Sugar   2 cups
Baking soda   1 tablespoon
Baking powder   3 tablespoons
Salt   4 teaspoons
Cinnamon   3 tablespoons
Ginger   3 tablespoons
Cloves   1 teaspoon
Margarine   1½ cups

Mix together dry ingredients. Cut in margarine with pastry blender or with mixer on low speed, until mixture is in very fine crumbs. Cover tightly and store in cool place. Makes about 2½ quarts of mix.

Gingerbread

Molasses   ¾ cup
Egg   1
Boiling water   ¾ cup
Gingerbread Mix (see Index)   3 cups
Whipped cream, ice cream, or sweetened cream cheese   topping

Beat molasses into egg, and stir in boiling water. Stir in Gingerbread Mix and beat well. Bake in greased and floured 9 by 9 by 2-inch pan at 350° for about 40 minutes. Serve warm with whipped cream.
Variation: For really festive gingerbread, sprinkle ½ cup of Crumbly Dutch Topping Mix (see Index) and ½ cup of chopped nuts on batter before baking.

Refrigerator Gingerbread Batter

This is even faster than the Gingerbread Mix, since the whole thing is made up ahead. Just spoon it into baking pans when you're ready to bake.

Margarine   1⅓ cups
Sugar   1⅓ cups
Eggs   4
Flour   4 cups unsifted and stirred
Baking soda   2 teaspoons
Cream of tartar   1 teaspoon
Cinnamon   2 teaspoons
Ginger   1 teaspoon
Cloves   1 teaspoon
Allspice   1 teaspoon
Mace or nutmeg   1 teaspoon
Molasses   1⅓ cups or
      Molasses and honey   1⅓ cups
Boiling water   2 cups

Cream together margarine and sugar until fluffy; beat in eggs. Stir dry ingredients together and add to creamed mixture alternately with molasses and boiling water; beat until smooth. Let batter cool, then cover and refrigerate. This will keep several days in the refrigerator. To bake, spoon batter (without stirring) into 2 greased and floured 9 by 9-inch baking pans. Bake at 350° for 35 to 45 minutes, or until done.

Refrigerator Chocolate Frosting

You can make this up ahead to frost graham crackers or cupcakes or any little thing.

Water   ½ cup
Cornstarch   2½ tablespoons
Salt   a pinch
Evaporated milk   1 5½-ounce can (⅔ cup)
Margarine   2 tablespoons
Semisweet chocolate chips   1 6-ounce package
Vanilla   1 teaspoon

Mix water and cornstarch in small pan; add salt, milk, and margarine. Cook over low heat until thick, stirring constantly. Add chocolate chips and stir until chocolate is melted. Remove from heat and stir in vanilla. Chill and store in tightly covered container in the refrigerator. Keeps for a week or more. Stir before using. Makes about 2 cups of frosting.

Make-Ahead Whipped Cream*

This whipped cream will keep at room temperature for several hours without turning watery, so it's good for the buffet table. It will keep in the refrigerator for up to a week. There are actually two ways of making it. One is if you have a little foresight, the other is if you don't.

Unflavored gelatin   1 teaspoon
Cold water   2 to 3 tablespoons
Whipping cream   1 cup, chilled
Powdered sugar   2 tablespoons
Vanilla   ½ teaspoon or
    Powdered vanilla   a pinch

Soak gelatin in cold water; heat carefully to dissolve. Add to whipping cream and stir. Refrigerate 1 hour to partially set. Add sugar and vanilla; whip until stiff. Serve at room temperature within 2 to 3 hours or refrigerate for later use. Stir before using, or scoop out with ice cream scoop without stirring. If you forget to prepare this ahead, just whip the cream with the sugar until it is in soft peaks, then add the dissolved gelatin mixture, beating it in all at once.
Note: If powdered vanilla is not available in your area, you can purchase it by mail from DeLaurenti Italian & International Market, 1435 First Avenue, Seattle, Washington 98101.
* Previously published in *The Green Tomato Cookbook* by Paula Simmons.

Ellen's Seasoning Salt

Salt   1¼ cups
Garlic powder   1½ teaspoons
Onion powder or granulated onion   1½ teaspoons
Celery salt   1 teaspoon
Paprika   1 tablespoon
Coarsely ground black pepper   2 tablespoons
Sugar   2 tablespoons
Dry mustard   1½ teaspoons
Curry powder   ¼ teaspoon

Mix together all ingredients; pack into shaker jars. Cover tightly and store in cool place. Makes about 1½ cups of seasoning salt.

Seasoning Salt for Lamb or Mutton

I understand this recipe originated many years ago in the Home Economics Department of Purdue University. I ran across it in Shepherd Magazine *maybe fifteen years ago. The popcorn salt dissolves instantly, so the seasoning doesn't fall off the meat.*

Fine plain popcorn salt   1 cup
Black pepper   1 teaspoon
Paprika   1 teaspoon
Ground ginger   ½ teaspoon
Dry mustard   ½ teaspoon
Poultry seasoning   ½ teaspoon
Cayenne pepper   ¼ to ⅓ teaspoon
Garlic salt   1 tablespoon or
    Garlic powder   2 teaspoons

Mix together all ingredients; pack into shaker jars. Seal tightly and store in cool place. Makes just over 1 cup of seasoning.

Salad Seasoning

Seasoning salt   1 tablespoon
Basil   1 tablespoon
Marjoram   1 tablespoon
Celery seed   1 tablespoon
Dillweed   1 tablespoon
Dried chives   1 tablespoon
Parsley flakes   1 tablespoon
Parmesan cheese   1 tablespoon grated
Freshly ground pepper   1 teaspoon
Sesame seeds   1½ tablespoons

Mix together all ingredients; pack into shaker jars and cover tightly. Makes just over ½ cup of seasoning.

Breads and Broth

You can build a hearty, satisfying meal around bread and soup made from homemade broth. I make mine in large quantities, so they're economical and always on hand.

Homemade Bread

We make our bread in huge batches, using a 16-quart stainless steel bowl for mixing the dough. We don't have an exact recipe. The yeast is the only ingredient that is measured exactly. The rest is just "by golly" and it always turns out fine. I put together all the ingredients, then my husband mixes and kneads it. At that point, I take over again and finish making the bread. So, get a big bowl and call your husband.

Dry yeast   5 packages
Lukewarm water   1 cup
Sugar, brown sugar, or honey   about ½ cup
Molasses   3 to 4 tablespoons
Oil   ¼ to ½ cup or
    Margarine or butter   ¼ to ½ cup, melted
Salt   2 tablespoons or less
Lukewarm water   2½ to 3 quarts or
    Apple juice, buttermilk, milk,
          tomato juice, or beer   2½ to 3 quarts, lukewarm
Rolled oats   2 to 3 cups (optional) or
    Wheat germ or bran   1 cup (optional)
Whole wheat, white, oat, soy, or rye flour   any combination, plus
    Gluten flour   2 cups (optional)
Oil   for brushing loaves (optional)

Soften yeast in lukewarm water. Combine next 6 ingredients; make sure they are lukewarm, then stir in softened yeast. Start adding flour, stirring in enough to make a fairly thick dough that leaves the side of the bowl. Turn dough out on floured surface and knead at least 10 minutes, or until dough becomes rather elastic. (Kneading develops the gluten, which makes the bread rise better. If it's not kneaded enough, the bread will have large holes instead of a fine texture.) Add more flour as needed. Place kneaded dough in very large oiled bowl, turning dough once to oil the top. Cover bowl (I clean out the mixing bowl and invert it over the oiled bowl) and leave in a warm place until doubled in bulk; depending on warmth, this should take from ¾ to 1½ hours. Actually, with so much dough, I can't bake all the loaves at once, so I raise ½ the loaves in a warm place, and keep the other ½ in a cool place until the first batch is in the oven. (An unheated hallway works well in the winter; 5 minutes in the refrigerator per loaf works well in summer.) When raised, punch dough down and turn out onto lightly floured surface. Cut off lumps to make loaves, and shape to fit ¾ of way to top of oiled pans. (Before putting each loaf into the oiled pan, you can cut slashes across the top of the dough and pat the top with oil. The slashes allow the bread to rise better and prevent unsightly bulges along the side of the top.) Allow the loaves to rise in a warm place until they are almost doubled in bulk, or until they are 1 inch above the sides of the pans. Bake at 350°, 30 to 35 minutes for 3 by 6-inch loaf pans, 40 to 45 minutes for 4 by 8-inch loaf pans, and 45 to 50 minutes for 5 by 9-inch loaf pans. After the loaves have baked 10 minutes, you can shift them around in the oven, moving those too close to the oven door to the back. After 10 minutes more, check to see how the loaves are browning; you may have to cover the whole batch with a sheet of foil to prevent overbrowning. When loaves are done, turn them out to cool on wire racks. Oil the tops for a tender crust. After bread is completely cooled, put each loaf in a plastic bag and store in the refrigerator. They can also be double-wrapped and frozen. Makes 10 to 15 loaves.

Variations: Add cardamom to bread when using buttermilk as liquid, cinnamon and nutmeg when using apple juice, caraway seeds when using tomato juice. Sprinkle sesame seeds into oiled bread pans before adding dough. Add dillweed, garlic, or onion powder. Add shredded cheese along with the flour.

Herb-Parmesan Bread

Homemade Bread dough
Oregano, thyme, basil, or other herbs   to taste
Seasoning salt   to taste
Parmesan cheese   to taste, grated
Water   to brush on loaves
Parmesan cheese   for sprinkling, grated or
    Sesame seeds   for sprinkling

Roll out lumps of dough. Combine herbs, seasoning salt, and cheese; spread over dough, then roll into loaves. Follow Homemade Bread recipe, but brush tops of loaves with water and sprinkle with cheese before baking.

Cinnamon Bread

Homemade Bread dough (see Index)
Butter or margarine   to taste, softened
Cinnamon   to taste
Sugar   to taste
Raisins or nuts   to taste

Roll out lumps of dough; spread with butter and sprinkle with cinnamon, sugar, and raisins. Roll dough into loaves. Follow Homemade Bread recipe, but sprinkle tops of loaves with cinnamon before baking.

English Muffins

Homemade Bread dough (see Index)
Cornmeal

Roll out dough on cornmeal-covered surface; cut into large rounds (a hamburger press works well). Allow rounds to rise, then carefully transfer with spatula to preheated 350° electric skillet. Cook, cornmeal side down, for 10 minutes, then turn and cook 10 minutes more. Cool on wire racks.

Anadama Cornmeal Bread

Cornmeal   2 cups
Cold water   3 cups
Boiling water   5 cups or more
Sugar, brown sugar, or honey   about ½ cup
Molasses   3 to 4 tablespoons
Oil   ¼ to ½ cup or
    Margarine or butter   ¼ to ½ cup, melted
Salt   2 tablespoons or less
Cold water   4 cups
Dry yeast   5 packages
Lukewarm water   1 cup
Flour
Cornmeal   for sprinkling on pans

Stir cornmeal into 3 cups cold water, then stir mixture into boiling water, along with sugar, molasses, oil, and salt. Set aside several minutes, then stir in 4 cups cold water. Be sure liquid is lukewarm, then stir in yeast that has been softened in lukewarm water. Stir in amount of flour called for in Homemade Bread recipe (see Index). Continue to follow recipe, but sprinkle bottoms of oiled pans with cornmeal before adding dough.

Depression Johnnycake

This is eggless!

Yellow cornmeal   1 cup
Baking soda   ½ teaspoon
Baking powder   ½ teaspoon
Salt   1 teaspoon
Buttermilk*   ⅔ cup
Cooking oil   2 tablespoons

Mix together dry ingredients, then stir in buttermilk and oil. If necessary, add a little more cornmeal so mixture is thick enough to hold its shape. Form into 8 mounds on oiled baking sheet and bake at 400° for 12 to 15 minutes, or until pale golden brown. Do not overbake. Makes 8 johnnycakes.
* You may substitute sour milk made from ⅔ cup milk mixed with 1 teaspoon vinegar and set aside 5 minutes.

Cheap and Easy Turkey Broth

When turkey drumsticks are on sale, I fill my shopping cart.

Turkey drumsticks

Place drumsticks (I usually do 16 or more at a time) in large shallow pans. Cover tightly with foil and bake on 2 oven shelves at 225° overnight. The foil keeps the juice from evaporating, and in the morning the pans will be swimming with broth and the turkey will be so done it will just fall off the bone. Pour off broth and refrigerate until fat can be skimmed off; reserve fat for sauce in Make-Ahead Turkey Casserole (see Index). While drumsticks are still warm, remove meat from bones; discard bones and skin. Save large pieces of meat for casseroles; use smaller tidbits in soup.
Variation: I add a container or two of my home-frozen vegetables (partially cooked, then frozen in the cooking water) to the broth, season it to taste, and presto—soup. You could also add barley, rice, or noodles if you don't plan to serve it with bread.

Salads, Side Dishes, and Pickles

My garden is rather chaotic; things crawl all over each other before the summer's over. The experts say, "Plant two feet apart," but that wastes a lot of space, so I don't listen to them, and everything ends up nudging everything else until you can't walk between them. But they do all right because they get plenty of nourishment from the barn—sheep manure and hay, six inches deep. We don't rototill either and we don't dig up the garden; we just spread on the mulch, dig little holes, and plunk in the plants. Easy. It produces more than we can eat, and with the plants so close together, I don't have to weed and I don't have to water so often, because the ground is well shaded even on hot days.

Wilted Lettuce Salad

When you're growing your own lettuce, and it's growing like crazy, all of a sudden you have more lettuce than you need, and if you don't use it, it will bolt and go to seed. This salad is one way to use up a heck of a lot of lettuce in a hurry.

Leaf lettuce   1 to 1½ quarts torn into bite-size pieces
Bacon strips   4, diced, fried crisp, and drained
Whole green onions   ¼ cup finely chopped
Vinegar   3 tablespoons
Water   1 tablespoon (unless lettuce is washed)
Sugar   1 teaspoon
Bacon drippings   2 tablespoons
Salt and pepper   to taste

Toss lettuce, bacon, and onions in a warmed salad bowl. Add vinegar, water, and sugar to hot bacon drippings in pan; bring to a boil and pour over the lettuce. Sprinkle with salt and pepper, toss well, and serve at once. Serves 4 to 6.

Sauerkraut Salad

This is something you can make in the winter with either homemade sauerkraut or inexpensive store-bought kraut. You don't have to buy the best kraut. With this recipe, you can use the cheapest, and it will taste just as good.

Vinegar ½ cup
Sugar ½ cup
Vegetable oil ¼ cup
Salt 1 teaspoon
Freshly ground pepper ½ teaspoon
Sauerkraut 1 16-ounce can
Medium onion 1, chopped
Small green pepper 1, chopped
Pimientos ½ 2-ounce bottle, drained and chopped (optional)
Water chestnuts 1 8-ounce can, sliced (optional)
Celery seed 1 teaspoon
Garlic salt ½ teaspoon

Combine the first 5 ingredients in small saucepan; bring to a boil, stirring to dissolve sugar. Put sauerkraut in colander, rinse with cold water, and drain. Place drained kraut in serving bowl and cover with hot vinegar mixture. Add remaining ingredients; mix well. Allow salad to cool, then cover bowl and refrigerate overnight before serving. Leftover salad will keep for a week or more in the refrigerator. Serves 4 to 6.

Hot Dutch Vegetable Salad

Alice Robinson, who gave me this recipe, says that any other vegetables may be substituted for those specified. I can't imagine any way it could taste better, though.

Fresh cabbage   2 to 3 cups chopped or
    Frozen cabbage   1 pint chopped or shredded, thawed
Carrots   1½ to 2 cups sliced
Peas   1 to 2 cups
Celery   1 to 2 cups thinly sliced diagonally
Green onions   2, chopped
French dressing   ⅓ to ½ cup
Sour cream or imitation sour cream   ¾ to 1 cup
Bacon strips   several, diced and fried crisp

Cook cabbage, carrots, peas, and celery separately, either steaming or cooking in very small quantities of water only until tender-crisp; drain well. Layer vegetables, 1 vegetable at a time, in 1 buttered 9 by 13-inch pan, 2 buttered 8 by 8-inch pans, or 1 buttered, preheated 9 by 12-inch Pyrex pan. Sprinkle with green onions, then with French dressing. Dot with sour cream and garnish with bacon. Serve at once or keep warm in 200° oven for 10 to 30 minutes. Serves 8.
Note: This may be made in advance, kept at room temperature, and heated in the oven just before serving.

Papaya Seed Salad Dressing

It seems a shame to throw papaya seeds away. I heard somebody say you could make dressing out of them, so I tried a little of this and a little of that, and wrote down what I tried. It makes an interesting, tasty dressing.

Fresh papaya seeds 1½ to 2 tablespoons
Vinegar ½ cup
Salad oil ¾ cup, or to taste
Lemon juice 2 tablespoons
Sugar ½ cup
Dried onion flakes or onion powder 1 teaspoon
Dry mustard 1 tablespoon
Paprika ½ teaspoon
Salt 1 tablespoon
Tarragon 1 teaspoon

Place all ingredients in blender and blend until papaya seeds, onion flakes, and tarragon are well chopped. Store in a covered container in refrigerator; use within 1 week. Makes about 1½ cups of dressing.

Lemon Butter for Asparagus or Broccoli

Lemon Butter is pretty fast to make and doesn't take anything that you don't ordinarily have on the kitchen shelf. My husband likes it on asparagus, but then he loves asparagus. Broccoli he gets a little tired of. When it's out of season in my garden and inexpensive in the store, I just go wild. I bring home lots. Well, he'd eat it every day of the week with Lemon Butter.

Margarine ¼ cup
Lemon juice of ½ lemon
Lemon peel of ½ lemon, grated
Sesame seeds 1 tablespoon
Sugar 1 teaspoon
Salt ¼ teaspoon
Garlic cloves 2, crushed and minced

Melt margarine in small saucepan and stir in remaining ingredients. Serve hot over cooked vegetables.

Scalloped Cabbage

My husband calls me "Mrs. Wiggs of the Cabbage Patch," because my cabbages are so happy. If we have too much wet and cool weather in the summer, the tomatoes don't ripen and some of the little squashes mold, but the cabbages just prosper. I plant an excess number of them because I figure the bugs are going to get a few. But once in a while every single plant makes it, and then we've really got cabbage. Sometimes I shred it and freeze it (after I've blanched and drained it). This recipe and the next one are good ways to use it, since you can't make salad out of it once it's been frozen.

Salt ¼ teaspoon
Sugar ¼ teaspoon
Fresh cabbage 3 cups coarsely shredded or
    Frozen cabbage 1 pint shredded, thawed
Boiling water
Medium Cheddar cheese 1 cup shredded
White Sauce
Bread crumbs ½ cup buttered
Freshly ground pepper a sprinkle

Add salt, sugar, and cabbage to small amount of boiling water and cook until just tender; drain well. Layer cabbage, cheese, and White Sauce in oiled 1-quart casserole. Cover with crumbs and sprinkle with pepper. Bake at 350° for 20 minutes, or until lightly browned. Serves 4 to 6.
Variation: Substitute cooked, drained, and chopped Swiss chard or cooked and drained spinach for cabbage; cover chard or spinach with layer of thinly sliced hard-cooked egg.

White Sauce

Margarine 3 tablespoons
Flour 3 tablespoons
Milk or skim milk 1½ cups
Salt ½ teaspoon

Melt margarine in small saucepan; mix in flour. Gradually stir in milk, add salt, and cook until thickened.

Quick and Creamy Cabbage

Fresh cabbage   3 cups shredded or
   Frozen cabbage   1 pint shredded, thawed
Salted boiling water
Cream cheese   1½ ounces, cut in pieces
Celery seed and/or onion powder   ⅛ teaspoon
Freshly ground pepper   a sprinkle
Salt   to taste

Add cabbage to small amount of salted boiling water; cover and cook 5 minutes, or until just tender. Drain off all but 1 tablespoon of the cooking water. Add cream cheese, celery seed, and pepper; stir until the cream cheese is melted. Add salt and serve at once. Serves 4.

Grandfather's Shaggy Dogs

Most of the vitamins in a potato are supposed to be in or very near the skin. Grandfather always said the skins had all the minerals, too. This recipe and the next take advantage of the skin's delicious taste as well.

Large potatoes   2, scrubbed and shredded
Leftover beef, pork, or other meat   ½ cup chopped
Egg   1, beaten
Onion   1 tablespoon finely chopped or
   Onion powder   ½ teaspoon
Salt   ½ teaspoon
Freshly ground pepper   a generous sprinkle
Biscuit Mix or Pancake Mix (see Index)   ¼ cup or
   Flour   ¼ cup and
   Baking powder   ½ teaspoon
Margarine   2 tablespoons, melted

Mix potatoes with meat, stir in next 5 ingredients, and mix well. Drop by tablespoonfuls into skillet and fry in margarine until golden brown on both sides. Serves 6.

Barbecue-Flavored Potato Wedges

Large potatoes   6 to 8, scrubbed
Cooking oil   ⅓ to ½ cup
Salt   1 teaspoon
Freshly ground pepper   ½ teaspoon
Paprika   ½ teaspoon
Garlic cloves   3, crushed and minced
Parmesan or Romano cheese   ¼ cup grated

Cut potatoes in half, then cut halves into 4 to 6 wedges each. (Smaller wedges bake faster—nice if you're in a hurry.) Mix together remaining ingredients, dip each wedge in mixture, and place on oiled cookie sheet skin sides down. Bake at 375° for 20 minutes, then drizzle remaining mixture over potatoes and bake another 15 to 25 minutes, or until potatoes are tender. Serves 6 to 8.
Note: If the rest of dinner is delayed, you can turn down the heat for the last ½ of the baking.

Festive Potato Balls

This is good for when you have two or three potatoes and they're all different sizes. It's an impressive dish for company, and you can reheat the little rascals if you have any left over.

Raw potatoes   any size, peeled
Cold water
Margarine   several tablespoons, melted
Parsley   garnish, finely chopped
Salt   to taste

Scoop out potato balls with a melon baller, using up the whole potato except for small scraps.* Place potato balls in saucepan and cover with cold water. Bring to a boil; boil 2 minutes. Pour off the water, which may be saved for soup or for making bread. Drain the potatoes for several minutes on paper towels. Pour margarine into shallow casserole, add potato balls, and stir gently to thoroughly coat potatoes. Bake at 375° until tender and lightly browned—25 to 35 minutes, depending on size of potato balls. Shake the casserole occasionally to stir the potatoes. Garnish with parsley, sprinkle with salt, and serve hot.
* Save the potato scraps, cook them separately until tender, and chop them for hash browns.

Make-Ahead Mashed Potato Casserole

Large potatoes   3 to 4, peeled and cubed
Sour cream   ¼ cup
Cream cheese   1 3-ounce package, softened and cubed
Salt and white pepper   to taste
Butter   to taste, melted

Boil potatoes until tender; drain. Mash potatoes, then add sour cream and cream cheese, beating until well mixed and fluffy. Spoon into oiled 1-quart casserole; brush with melted butter. You may cover and refrigerate the casserole for several hours or several days at this point. To serve, bake at 350° for 30 to 40 minutes, or until very hot and delicately browned. Serves 4.
Note: If mixture seems runny beat in an egg.

Tender Soybeans

Soybeans are an inexpensive source of protein, but many of us won't bother with them, because even with all the soaking and cooking, they're still not as tender as we thought they were going to be. I soak them and then freeze them. Since they don't take so long to cook after they've been frozen and since I always have some in the freezer, it's simple to prepare them on short notice and add them to stretch a meal.

Dried soybeans   1 cup
Chicken bouillon granules   1 tablespoon or
     Chicken bouillon cubes   3
Boiling water   ¼ cup
Cold water   2 cups
Butter, margarine, or oil   1 tablespoon

Place soybeans in large bowl or tapered quart jar. Dissolve bouillon in boiling water, add to cold water, and pour over beans. Soak overnight. Cover bowl or place lid on jar and place soaked beans and liquid in freezer. Freeze solid until you are ready to use the soybeans, then thaw them and place beans and soaking liquid in pressure cooker with lid off.* Bring to a boil; skim off foam. Add butter; pressure cook for 20 minutes at 15 pounds pressure. The beans will be very tender and may be served hot with butter or catsup. Leftovers may be refrigerated and reheated. Serves 4.
* Never fill a pressure cooker more than ½ full of soybeans.

Refrigerator Cucumbers

This is a way of making pickles without pickling. I use any kind of cucumber. Some have to be peeled and some don't, some are long and some are short; it doesn't matter. I make up a triple amount, or more, of the syrup, and put this in a gallon jar in the refrigerator. When I get more cucumbers, I slice, salt, and drain them, then mix them into the ones already in the jar. They will keep quite crisp for a year in the refrigerator. Just take a handful out whenever you need them.

Cucumbers   5 to 8 cups thinly sliced
Onions   1 cup sliced
Green peppers   1 cup thinly sliced (optional)
Pickling salt   2 to 3 tablespoons
Sugar   1½ cups
Vinegar   1 cup
Celery seed   1 tablespoon

Sprinkle sliced vegetables with salt; let them drain for 1 hour. Combine sugar, vinegar, and celery seed in small saucepan; heat to dissolve sugar, then chill. Place the vegetables in glass jars and cover with syrup. Cover tightly and refrigerate at least 24 hours before eating.

Main Dishes

I don't have any problem cooking steaks or chops or roasts without .
recipes, but over the years, I have found some main dishes with such
special tastes that I didn't want to forget how to duplicate them. So I wrote
them down.

Oriental Casserole

This is an easy casserole. (I don't see any reason for making a casserole unless it is easy.)

Ground beef or lamb 1 pound
Frozen peas 1 12-ounce package, thawed
Celery 2 cups thinly sliced
Salt ½ teaspoon
Freshly ground pepper ¼ teaspoon
Small onion 1, finely chopped
**Condensed cream of mushroom, cream of celery,
    or cream of chicken soup** 1 10½-ounce can
Potato chips ½ 1¼-ounce package, crushed

Brown meat, drain off fat, and turn into casserole or loaf pan. Spread peas over meat, then spread celery; sprinkle with salt and pepper. Mix onion into soup, and spread over all. Sprinkle with potato chips and bake 30 minutes at 375°. Serves 4. Any leftovers are good reheated.

Corn-Stuffed Pepper Rings

Large green peppers 4
Ground beef 1 pound
Tomatoes 1 14½-ounce can
Whole kernel corn 1 8½-ounce can, drained
Olives 1 2¼-ounce can, drained and sliced
Salt 1 teaspoon
Freshly ground pepper ½ teaspoon
Garlic powder ¼ teaspoon
Tabasco sauce several drops (optional)
Medium Cheddar cheese 8 chunks, for topping

Cut both ends off each pepper; reserve ends for other uses. Remove seeds and slice each pepper into 2 large rings. Sauté ground beef until lightly browned; drain off fat. Stir next 7 ingredients into beef and heat through. Place pepper rings in shallow greased pan; fill them with meat mixture, putting any excess around the rings. Cover with foil and bake at 350° for 45 minutes. Remove foil, put a chunk of cheese on top of each ring, and bake uncovered 10 minutes more. Serves 4.

Tortilla Pie*

If you're making dinner for four to six people, this is easier than fixing separate little tortillas or tacos or something else. Casseroles like this are a good idea when you have someone coming. You can put the pie in the oven and you won't have to keep looking at it or worry about making several dishes all come out at the same time.

Ground beef or lamb 1½ pounds
Onion ½ cup chopped
Medium green pepper 1, chopped
Tomato sauce 1 15-ounce can
Salt ½ teaspoon, or to taste
Coarsely ground pepper 1 teaspoon
Corn chips 1½ cups crushed
Medium Cheddar cheese 1 cup shredded
Cheddar cheese 6 thin slices

Sauté meat, onion, and green pepper until meat has lost its redness, separating with a fork as it cooks. Pour off fat; stir in tomato sauce and seasonings. In shallow casserole, place ⅓ of corn chips, then ½ the meat mixture and ½ the shredded cheese. Repeat layers and top with remaining corn chips. Bake 30 minutes at 350°, then top with cheese slices and bake about 5 minutes more. Serves 4 to 6. Good with a green salad.
* From *Raising Sheep the Modern Way* by Paula Simmons.

Vi's Tamale Pie

The meat mixture is sufficient for two pies, so you can freeze half for later use. Next time, all you'll have to do is put your cornmeal crust together.

Ground beef or lamb   3 pounds
Green pepper   1, chopped
Large onion   1, chopped
Tomatoes   1 15-ounce can
Tomato sauce   1 15-ounce can
Tomato paste   1 6-ounce can (optional)
Ripe olives   1 cup sliced
Sugar   2 teaspoons
Salt   1 teaspoon, or to taste
Chili powder   1 tablespoon
Ground cumin   1 tablespoon
Cayenne   to taste (optional)
Cornmeal Crust
Cheddar cheese   ½ cup shredded

Sauté meat, green pepper, and onion until meat loses its redness. Add next 8 ingredients and simmer 15 minutes, then taste for seasoning, adding more chili powder if desired. Add cayenne if you like it hot. Divide meat mixture, freezing ½ for later use. Spread remaining meat mixture over Cornmeal Crust. Decorate the edges with small spoonfuls of ½ cup of cornmeal mixture you set aside. Bake 30 minutes at 350°; spread cheese on top and bake 5 minutes more. Set aside for 10 minutes before serving. Serves 6.

Cornmeal Crust

Yellow cornmeal   1 cup
Cold water   1 cup
Boiling water   1 cup
Salt   1 teaspoon

Mix cornmeal with cold water, then stir it into boiling water along with salt. Cook slowly, stirring constantly, until thick. Set aside ½ cup of cornmeal; spread remaining cornmeal in large shallow baking dish.

Stuart Special

Frozen spinach   1 10-ounce package, thawed or
   Fresh spinach   1 pound, cooked and chopped
Lean ground beef   1 pound
Onion   1 cup chopped
Eggs   2, slightly beaten
Salt   ½ teaspoon
Pepper   a sprinkle

Drain spinach in strainer, then on paper towels; set aside. Sauté beef and onion until meat is cooked and onion is tender. Add spinach to meat mixture and mix well. Add the remaining ingredients, stir, and cook until eggs are completely done. Serves 4.

Hamburger Collopse

This is like a slumgullion or a poorly organized goulash.

Lean ground beef   1 pound
Thyme   ½ teaspoon
Salt and pepper   to taste
Flour   ½ cup
Onions   2, sliced
Water
Rice, mashed potatoes, or noodles   4 servings

Sauté meat, stirring so it forms a loose mixture. Add seasonings. Sift or sprinkle flour over all, then top with onions. Cover with water to level of meat, and simmer 30 to 40 minutes. Serve over rice. Serves 4.

Savory Stew Meat

This makes an absolutely delicious meal in under thirty minutes. You can even skip browning the meat if you're in a rush.

Fat or oil   2 tablespoons
Stew meat, chuck steak, or chuck roast*   1½ to 2 pounds, cubed
Garlic cloves   4, minced
Catsup   ½ cup
Worcestershire sauce   2 teaspoons
Water   2 tablespoons
Salt and pepper   to taste
Rice or noodles   4 to 6 servings

Heat pressure cooker and add fat. Brown meat in hot fat. Combine the next 5 ingredients and pour over meat. Put the top on the pressure cooker at once, allow steam to flow from vent to release air, and put on indicator valve. Cook 20 minutes at 15 pounds pressure, with heat turned down low so meat won't scorch. Remove from heat and let pressure reduce completely. Serve with rice. Serves 4 to 6.
* Any suitable meat can be used.

Pot Roast with Honey

Kitchen Bouquet   1 tablespoon
Honey   1 tablespoon
Boneless pot roast   any size
Large onion   1, chopped
Salt and pepper   to taste
Water   ½ cup
Vegetables   (optional)

Mix Kitchen Bouquet and honey in Dutch oven. Add pot roast and turn over in mixture until coated. Brown roast on each side for 10 minutes, then add remaining ingredients. Cook over very low heat or bake at 225° until very tender. (May also be cooked all day or overnight in electric slow-cooking pot.) Drain off pan juices and chill until fat can be skimmed off. Reheat roast in juice, adding vegetables as desired and simmering until they are done. Serves 2 to 3 per pound of meat.
Note: For easy serving, cut roast into thick slices and tie with string before cooking.

Pot Roast in Beer

Boneless pot roast   any size
Cooking oil   1 tablespoon
Beer   1 12-ounce bottle
Large onion   1, chopped
Celery   1 cup chopped
Tomatoes   1 16-ounce can
Zucchini   1 cup shredded
Garlic cloves   3 to 4, crushed
Salt and pepper   to taste
Flour   2 tablespoons (optional)
Noodles

Brown pot roast on all sides in hot oil. Add next 7 ingredients and simmer over very low heat or bake at 300° for several hours, or until meat is very tender. Pour off liquid and skim off fat. Blend vegetables and liquid in blender, adding flour for thicker gravy, then reheat and simmer several minutes. Serve over noodles. Serves 2 to 3 per pound of meat.

Variation: This is very festive garnished with sliced sautéed mushrooms.

Note: For easy serving, cut roast into thick slices and tie with string before cooking.

Cabbage Buns

Pork or beef sausage   ¾ to 1 pound or
    Ground beef, lamb, or mutton   ¾ to 1 pound
Small onion   1, chopped
Salt   to taste
Freshly ground pepper   very generous pinch
Fresh or frozen cabbage   2 cups cooked and shredded or
    Sauerkraut   2 cups, rinsed and drained
Homemade Bread dough (see Index)   enough for 2 loaves
Oil or butter   for brushing

Lightly sauté sausage and onion, cooking just until meat loses redness. Add seasonings, then mix in cabbage. Set aside. Roll out dough to ¼-inch thickness, then cut into 4-inch squares or circles. Place 2 or 3 tablespoons of filling on dough, then fold over and seal like a turnover or pinch corners together in center. Place buns upside down on cookie sheet and bake 30 minutes at 350° or 20 minutes at 375°. Remove buns to wire rack, brush with oil, and cool 5 minutes before serving. Leftover buns may be reheated in a paper sack. Makes 1½ to 2 dozen.

Ham Casserole

No matter what you do with a ham, there's always a little bit left—chunks and pieces that don't look like much. This casserole combines the ham with bread (homemade is best), and comes out of the oven very edible and very reheatable.

Whole wheat bread 6 slices
Medium Cheddar cheese 1½ cups, shredded
Celery 2 cups diagonally sliced and cooked
Ham 2 cups diced, chopped, or chunked
Milk or skim milk 2 cups
Eggs 4, beaten
Seasoning salt ½ teaspoon
Coarsely ground pepper ½ teaspoon
Garlic powder ¼ teaspoon
Dried minced onion 1 tablespoon or
    Fresh onion 2 tablespoons chopped

With doughnut or cookie cutter, cut a 2- to 3-inch round from the center of each bread slice. Crumble the rest of the bread into the bottom of a shallow 1½-quart casserole. Cover with a layer of cheese, then a layer of celery, then ham. Place the bread rounds on top. Combine the remaining ingredients and pour over all. Refrigerate at least 1 hour, then bake at 350° for 1 hour, or until firm. Serves 6.

Make-Ahead Quiche

Pie shell   9-inch, unbaked, edges fluted
Bacon strips or bacon ends   ½ pound or less, fried crisp and
   well drained or
      Ham   ½ pound or less, sliced or chopped
Eggs   3, slightly beaten
Milk   1⅔ cups or
      Evaporated milk or evaporated skim milk   1 13-ounce can
Onion salt   1 teaspoon
Cayenne   a pinch
Nutmeg   a pinch
Swiss or jack cheese   1 cup shredded
Flour   1 tablespoon

Sprinkle pie shell with bacon. Combine remaining ingredients, mixing well. The quiche makings may be refrigerated for up to 10 hours. Store filling in covered bowl; place pie shell in plastic bag or cover with plastic wrap. Remove filling from refrigerator ½ hour before baking. When ready to bake, pour filling over bacon in pie shell; bake 10 minutes at 425°, then reduce heat to 350° and bake 20 to 25 minutes more, or until knife inserted halfway between center and edge of quiche comes out clean. Cool 10 to 15 minutes on wire rack before serving. To bake quiche immediately, bake pie shell 6 to 8 minutes at 450° while you are mixing the filling. Sprinkle shell with bacon, add filling, and bake at 350° for 25 to 35 minutes, or until done.
Variations: For Turkey Quiche, substitute 1 cup cubed turkey for bacon, substitute one ⅞-ounce package of turkey gravy mix for flour, and sprinkle cheese over filling before baking instead of adding to egg mixture. For Spicy Italian Quiche, substitute ¾ cup chopped pepperoni or salami for bacon, and stir ½ teaspoon oregano and 1 chopped green onion into egg mixture.

Oregon Lamb

Four of my friends served this for lunch during a spinners' workshop at Chiloquin, Oregon, and it immediately became my favorite lamb recipe. It makes quite a bit, and requires a 3½-quart electric slow-cooking pot.

Flour   3 tablespoons
Dry mustard   1 teaspoon
Salt   1 teaspoon
Coarsely ground pepper   ½ teaspoon
Lamb shanks   4, split or
    Lamb neck   3 to 4 pounds, sliced or
    Lamb steaks, chops, or shoulder roast   2 to 3 pounds
Oil   for browning
Consommé   1 10½-ounce can
Condensed cream of mushroom soup   1 10½-ounce can
Worcestershire sauce   1 tablespoon
Kitchen Bouquet   1 tablespoon
Garlic powder   ⅛ teaspoon
Curry powder   ½ teaspoon
White wine   ½ cup
Rice, noodles, or potatoes   4 to 6 servings

Put flour, mustard, salt and pepper in a paper bag. Add lamb and shake to coat. Brown lamb in hot oil in nonstick skillet and place in slow-cooking pot. Combine all remaining ingredients except rice, and add to pot; sauce should cover about ¾ of the meat. Cook 1 hour on high, then cook on low for 6 to 8 hours, or until lamb is extremely well done. Serve at once, or pour off all liquid and chill it until the fat can be skimmed off. Pour remaining liquid back over meat and reheat. Serve on rice. Serves 4 to 6.

Lamb Curry

Lamb ribs or lamb breast are moderately priced cuts of meat at the market and "what-can-I-do-with-it" cuts if you raise your own. Here's a delicious way to use them.

Lamb ribs or lamb breast   2 pounds
Water   1 cup
Large onion   1, chopped
Curry powder   1 tablespoon, or to taste
Reserved lamb liquid or water   1 cup
Salt   1 teaspoon
Ground fenugreek or ground cumin   1 teaspoon
Raisins   1 tablespoon
Apple   1, peeled and chopped
Rice   4 to 6 servings
**Chutney, ground coconut, raisins, chopped nuts or
    sunflower seeds, chopped green onions, chopped hard-cooked
    eggs, chopped green pepper, sautéed banana slices**   side dishes

Pressure cook lamb with water for 20 minutes at 15 pounds pressure; cool to reduce pressure. Drain off liquid and chill, then skim off fat. Let meat cool until it can be handled comfortably, then separate lean pieces from fat, bone, and skin. Place lean tidbits in saucepan with onion and curry powder, plus 1 tablespoon of lamb liquid; sauté until onion is transparent. Add remaining lamb liquid, plus salt, fenugreek, raisins, and apple; simmer 20 minutes. Set aside at room temperature for 1 hour, then reheat and serve over rice, accompanied by side dishes. Serves 4.

Zesty Mongolian Chicken

If you have the chicken boned and cubed ahead of time, and the sauce already mixed, this dish takes only about six minutes to cook from start to finish.

Chicken breasts 2, skinned, boned, and in 1-inch cubes
Cornstarch ¼ cup
Cooking oil 2 tablespoons
Garlic cloves 4, crushed and minced
Soy sauce ⅓ cup
Water ¼ cup
Sugar 1 teaspoon
Vinegar 1½ tablespoons
Green onions ⅓ cup chopped
Cayenne a pinch (optional)

Shake chicken cubes in paper bag with cornstarch. Heat oil in nonstick skillet; add chicken and garlic, and stir fry until lightly browned. Combine soy sauce, water, sugar, and vinegar; add to chicken and stir. Cover and cook several minutes, or until chicken is cooked through and sauce is absorbed. Add onions and cayenne; stir fry another 2 minutes. Serves 4.

Buttermilk Baked Chicken

I make buttermilk by mixing up a gallon of powdered milk and adding about two cups of buttermilk to it. I leave it out at room temperature and the next day the whole thing has turned to buttermilk. I save a cup of it for the next batch, then, if I have a lot of freezer space, I put the whole thing in the freezer in half-gallon containers to use later for bread. (It's great for baking bread.)

Buttermilk 1 cup
Flour ¾ cup
Salt ½ teaspoon
Pepper ½ teaspoon
Rosemary or thyme ½ teaspoon, crumbled
Large fryer 1, cut in serving pieces

Pour buttermilk into shallow pan. Combine flour and seasonings in plastic bag. Dip chicken into buttermilk, then shake in flour mixture. (Repeat once for a thicker coating.) Place chicken on a wire rack for 30 minutes or more, to allow the coating to set. Bake on oiled broiler rack at 375° for about 1 hour. If chicken gets too brown, cover loosely with foil for the last 20 minutes. You may use the remaining flour and buttermilk for making gravy. Serves 4.

Make-Ahead Turkey Casserole

This is a good way to use up holiday leftovers or supermarket specials.

Regular dressing mix   1 6-ounce package
Cornmeal dressing mix   1 6-ounce package
Onion   ½ cup finely chopped
Celery   1 cup chopped
Turkey Cream Sauce
Turkey   2 to 3 cups cooked, boned, and chopped or sliced
Bread crumbs   buttered

Prepare mixes according to directions, adding onion and celery. Spray foil pans, of sizes appropriate to number of servings planned, with nonstick lecithin spray. Place a layer of dressing in each pan, cover with layer of Turkey Cream Sauce and layer of turkey. Add another layer of dressing and a layer of sauce. Sprinkle with crumbs. Bake at 400° for 30 minutes, or until top is browned and mixture is bubbling. To freeze for later use, chill casseroles, then cover tightly with foil, place in plastic bags, label, and freeze. Thaw before baking or bake frozen.
Note: You may substitute a large batch of homemade stuffing for the prepared dressings.

Turkey Cream Sauce

Flour   1 cup
Turkey fat   1 cup or
    Turkey fat and butter or margarine   1 cup
Cheap and Easy Turkey Broth (see Index)   4 cups
Milk or skim milk   1 cup
Chicken bouillon cubes   2
Salt   1 teaspoon, or to taste
Eggs   4, beaten

In saucepan, add flour to turkey fat. Heat broth with milk and bouillon cubes; add to flour mixture. Cook over very low heat until sauce thickens, stirring constantly. Add salt. Stir hot mixture into eggs, a little at a time to prevent curdling. Return sauce to pan and cook slowly for 5 minutes, stirring constantly, then set sauce aside to cool.

Elaine's Baked Seashore Salad

This makes a lot, so it's good for potlucks, and you can serve it hot, cold, or reheated. Elaine says the original recipe called for crab, but it's more economical and just as good with tuna. Start this the day before you plan to serve it.

White bread 8 slices, crusts trimmed
Tuna 2 6½-ounce cans, drained and flaked
Mayonnaise ½ cup
Celery 1 cup minced
Medium onion 1, minced
Green pepper 1, chopped
Eggs 4, beaten
Milk 3 cups
Worcestershire sauce 1 teaspoon
Condensed cream of mushroom soup 1 10½-ounce can
Medium Cheddar cheese ½ cup grated

Cube bread and place ½ the cubes in the bottom of an ungreased 9 by 13-inch pan or casserole. Combine the next 5 ingredients; spoon over bread. Cover with remaining bread cubes. Combine eggs, milk, and Worcestershire sauce; pour over all. Cover pan with foil or plastic wrap, and refrigerate overnight. Remove pan from refrigerator 1 hour before baking. Bake uncovered for 15 minutes at 350° (325° for Pyrex). Spoon soup over casserole, sprinkle with cheese, and lower heat to 325° (300° for Pyrex); bake 1 hour longer. Serves 8; or 4, leaving good leftovers.

Clam Rarebit

This is a quick little thing you can fix for lunch on those days when you're wondering what to make. It's also a good impromptu snack, because you are likely to have the ingredients on hand.

Sharp Cheddar cheese   2 ounces, shredded
Clams   1 10-ounce can, minced or chopped,
     broth drained and reserved
Worcestershire sauce   ½ teaspoon
Dry mustard   ½ teaspoon
Bread   2 slices, toasted

Place cheese in top of double boiler. Add clam broth, Worcestershire sauce, and mustard. Heat over boiling water, stirring constantly, until cheese is melted and smooth. Stir in clams, remove from heat, and continue stirring for 1 minute. Serve on toast. Serves 2.

Desserts, Drinks, and Treats

This chapter includes my favorite desserts. I like desserts, but not ones that are too sweet. I usually cut the sugar to half what the original recipe calls for, and it still turns out quite nicely.

Wallbanger Gelatin*

Like its namesake, this gelatin has a "kick." You can make it in a flat pan and cut it into squares to serve as a salad, or let it set in liqueur glasses or goblets for dessert. I like recipes like this that are so doggone easy—and everyone says "wow!"

Unflavored gelatin   1 tablespoon
Cold water   ½ cup
Frozen concentrated orange juice   ⅔ cup, thawed
Water   ½ cup
Homemade Italiano Liqueur (see Index)   ⅓ cup
Whipped cream or mayonnaise   topping

Soak gelatin in cold water, then heat gently to dissolve gelatin. Mix together orange juice, water, and Homemade Italiano; add to gelatin and mix well. Pour into dessert glasses or into 8 by 8-inch pan, and chill until firm. Top with whipped cream for dessert, with mayonnaise for salad.
* Published in the Seattle *Post-Intelligencer* as "My Favorite Recipe."

Instant Chocolate Mousse*

This is my version of chocolate mousse, fast and easy. Usually, when you're fixing a dessert, you have to find a place in your refrigerator to put six dessert glasses; you almost have to clean off a whole shelf to find that much room. This is something that must not be refrigerated. You can make it before supper and let it sit right there on the counter at room temperature, then serve it when you're through eating. Just make sure you have the dessert glasses ready; if you don't move fast when you make it, you'll have to take it out of the blender with a spoon. This tastes very rich, by the way, even though it's not.

Unflavored gelatin   2 tablespoons
Cold water   1 cup
Chocolate chips   1 cup
Milk   ½ cup
Powdered skim milk   ½ cup
Ice cubes   5 to 7, crushed

Have 6 dessert glasses ready *before* you start dessert. In small saucepan, soften gelatin in cold water for a few minutes, then heat, stirring constantly, to dissolve gelatin. Pour into blender container, add chocolate chips, and blend. Add liquid and powdered milk; blend. Add crushed ice cubes 1 at a time, making sure each cube is completely blended into mixture before adding the next (otherwise you may have ice crystals in the finished dessert). When mixture starts to thicken, pour *quickly* into dessert glasses. It will be too thick to pour if you hesitate. Serve at once or within 1 hour. Do *not* make this way ahead and refrigerate, or it will be too tough to eat. Serves 6.

* This recipe was originally printed in the *Bainbridge Arts and Crafts Starving Artists Cook Book*, published by Bainbridge Island Arts and Crafts, Inc.

Blackberry Juice Tapioca

Tapioca ¼ cup
Blackberry juice* 2½ cups
Salt a pinch
Sugar ¼ to ½ cup
Cream or whipped cream topping

In saucepan, mix together all ingredients and set aside for 5 minutes, then bring to a boil, stirring constantly. Remove from heat and cool 10 minutes, then spoon into dessert glasses. Cool 10 minutes more to serve warm, or chill. Serve with cream.

* I use blackberry juice made in the steam juicer (see Index).

Fruit Pudding I

Home-canned peaches or pears 1 pint, with syrup or
    Canned peaches, pears, or fruit cocktail 1 17-ounce can
Flour 1 cup
Sugar ½ cup
Brown sugar ⅓ cup
Salt ½ teaspoon
Baking powder 1½ teaspoons
Egg 1
Walnuts ½ cup chopped
Brown sugar ¼ cup

Drain fruit, reserving ¼ cup syrup. Chop fruit and set aside. Mix together dry ingredients, then add egg and reserved fruit syrup. Stir in chopped fruit and nuts; mix well. Pour into greased 9 by 9-inch baking pan, and sprinkle with ¼ cup brown sugar. Bake at 325° for 45 to 60 minutes.

Fruit Pudding II

Flour 1 cup unsifted
Sugar 1 cup
Cinnamon 1 teaspoon or
    Cinnamon ½ teaspoon and
    Nutmeg ½ teaspoon
Salt a pinch
Baking soda 1¼ teaspoons
Nuts ½ cup chopped
Canned sliced peaches, pears, or cherries 1 pint, well drained
Egg 1, beaten
Cooking oil 2 teaspoons
Whipped cream topping

Mix dry ingredients together, then add remaining ingredients and mix.
Wait several minutes, then remix. If batter seems too wet, add a bit more
flour. Spoon into 8 by 8-inch pan and bake at 350° for 30 to 40 minutes, or
until done. Top should be soft and browned, but should not feel liquidy
underneath. Serve warm or cold with whipped cream.
Note: This not only stays moist for several days, it may even get a little
more moist, depending on the fruit used in it.

Nut Squares

If you get a good buy on walnuts, don't be afraid to make a pig of yourself. When I get a deal on twenty-five pounds, I freeze most of them. It's the only way to keep nuts fresh over a long period of time, and they'll keep indefinitely if you wrap them well first.

Egg 1
Brown sugar 1 cup
Vanilla 1¼ teaspoons
Flour ½ cup unsifted
Baking soda ½ teaspoon
Salt a pinch
Walnuts 1½ cups chopped
Ice cream topping (optional)

Stir together the egg, brown sugar, and vanilla until there are no brown sugar lumps. Stir in the dry ingredients, then the walnuts. Spread in greased 8 by 8-inch pan and bake at 350° for 18 to 20 minutes, or until top is lightly browned. The center will still be slightly soft. Cool in pan before cutting into squares. Serve topped with ice cream for dessert or use as a bar cookie.

Easy Saucepan Bars

Margarine ⅔ cup
Brown sugar 1 pound
Vanilla 1½ teaspoons
Eggs 3
Flour 2 cups unsifted
Baking powder 2 teaspoons
Salt ¼ teaspoon
Chocolate chips 1 6-ounce package, or 1 cup
Nuts ½ cup chopped

Melt margarine in large saucepan; remove from heat and add brown sugar and vanilla; mix well. Allow mixture to cool to lukewarm. Stir in eggs, then dry ingredients, then chocolate chips and nuts. Spread batter in greased and floured 9 by 13-inch pan; bake at 350° for 25 to 35 minutes, or until done. Cool and cut into squares.

Bonnie's Chocolate Marble Bars

This is a fast way to make nice marbled bar cookies or cake. Remember: the smaller the pan, the thicker the bar, so adjust the cooking time accordingly.

Margarine   ½ cup
Sugar   ⅓ cup
Brown sugar   ⅓ cup
Egg   1
Vanilla   1 teaspoon
Flour   1 cup unsifted
Baking soda   1 teaspoon
Salt   1 teaspoon
Nuts   ½ cup chopped
Semisweet chocolate chips   1 6-ounce package, or 1 cup

Beat margarine, sugars, and egg together until fluffy; add vanilla. Stir dry ingredients together, then stir into sugar mixture. Mix in nuts and spread batter evenly in 11¼ by 7¼-inch pan or several small foil pans. Sprinkle chocolate chips on top, then place in 350° oven for 1 minute, or until chips are softened. Remove pan and run knife through batter to marble it with chocolate. Bake at 350° for 12 to 15 minutes. Cool and cut into bars.

Coconut-Fruit Bars

This is a bit like my two fruit puddings, except it's not as moist — it's definitely a bar cookie.

Canned peaches or pears   1 pint, with syrup
Eggs   2
Sugar   1 cup
Flour   2¼ cups unsifted
Salt   ½ teaspoon
Baking soda   1½ teaspoons
Vanilla   1 teaspoon
Nuts   ⅓ cup chopped or
    Almonds   ⅓ cup sliced
Shredded or flaked coconut   1 cup

Dice fruit; set aside in syrup. Beat eggs and sugar together until fluffy. Add fruit along with flour, salt, baking soda, and vanilla; stir or beat only until blended. Pour into greased and floured 10 by 15-inch pan (or into 9 by 13-inch pan plus 6 cupcake tins); sprinkle with nuts and coconut. Bake at 350° for 20 to 25 minutes (a little less for cupcakes), or until lightly browned and done.

Chocolate Molasses Bars

Margarine   ½ cup
Brown sugar   ⅔ cup
Molasses   ¼ cup
Vanilla   1¼ teaspoons
Eggs   2
Flour   1 cup
Salt   a pinch
Shredded coconut   1 cup
Semisweet chocolate chips   ⅔ cup

Beat margarine and brown sugar together until fluffy, then beat in molasses, vanilla, and eggs. Mix in flour and salt, then stir in coconut. Bake in greased and floured 9 by 9-inch baking pan at 350° for 25 minutes. Remove from oven, sprinkle with chocolate chips, and return to oven for a minute to soften chocolate. Spread softened chips around to make frosting. To cut into neat squares, mark off squares in frosting while it is still warm. Cut when cool.

Violet's Cream Cheese Bars

Walnuts   ½ cup chopped
Special Dry Piecrust Mix (see Index)   1½ cups
Neufchâtel cheese   1 8-ounce package, at room temperature
Sugar   ¼ cup
Egg   1
Vanilla   ½ teaspoon
Lemon juice   1 teaspoon
Lemon peel   1 teaspoon grated or
    Powdered lemon peel   1 teaspoon

Stir nuts into piecrust mix; spread ⅔ of mixture in 8 by 8 by 2-inch baking pan and press down firmly. Bake at 350° for 12 to 15 minutes, or until lightly browned. Meanwhile, beat remaining ingredients together until very smooth. Pour mixture over hot crust, spreading evenly. Cover with remaining crust mixture, patting it down. Bake at 350° for 25 minutes; cool well, then refrigerate. Serve cold.
Note: These can be frozen if you first cut them, chill, then wrap in plastic and foil.

Saucepan Fudge Brownies

Margarine ⅓ cup
Sugar ½ cup
Water 2 tablespoons
Vanilla 1½ teaspoons
Chocolate chips 1 6-ounce package, or 1 cup
Eggs 2
Flour ¾ cup unsifted
Baking soda ¼ teaspoon
Salt a pinch
Nuts ½ cup chopped

Place margarine, sugar, and water in saucepan; bring to a boil, stirring constantly. Remove from heat, and stir in vanilla and chocolate chips. Beat until smooth, then cool slightly. Stir in eggs, then the flour, baking soda, and salt. Stir in ½ the nuts and pour batter into greased 8 by 8-inch pan. Sprinkle with remaining nuts and bake at 325° for 25 minutes, or until edges are firm and top is shiny. Cool and cut into squares.
Note: If you decide to double the recipe, do *not* bake in a larger pan: the outside edges get too well done before the center is cooked. Use two 8 by 8-inch pans or several small foil pans.

Quick Blackberry Juice Pie

Blackberry juice* 1½ cups
Lemon juice 1 tablespoon
Sugar ⅓ to ½ cup
Salt a pinch
Cornstarch ¼ cup
Blackberry juice or water ½ cup
Margarine or butter 2 tablespoons
Vanilla 2 teaspoons
Pie shell 8- or 9-inch, baked
Whipped cream or ice cream topping

In saucepan, combine blackberry juice, lemon juice, sugar, and salt; bring to a boil. Dissolve cornstarch in ½ cup blackberry juice and add to juice in saucepan; boil 3 minutes or until mixture is thick and clear, stirring constantly. Remove from heat and stir in margarine and vanilla. Cool slightly and spoon into pie shell. Chill several hours; serve with whipped cream.
* I use blackberry juice made in the steam juicer (see Index).

Rich Blueberry Pie

In this recipe, a few of the blueberries are cooked in the filling and the rest are added once the filling is thick, so it tastes very fresh. I quite often use frozen blueberries; when the blueberries themselves are already quite cold, the filling cools down in a hurry, making this a really fast pie.

Special Dry Piecrust Mix (see Index)   for 1 9-inch pie shell
Sugar   ½ cup
Cornstarch   2 tablespoons
Nutmeg   ¼ teaspoon
Water   1 tablespoon
Fresh blueberries   3 cups or
    Frozen blueberries   3 cups, well drained and dried
Lemon juice   1 teaspoon
Lemon peel   1 teaspoon grated
Sweetened whipped cream   topping

Press piecrust mix into 9-inch pie tin or tart pan. Bake at 400° for 10 to 12 minutes, or until pale brown; cool. Mix sugar, cornstarch, and nutmeg in saucepan. Stir in water and 1 cup of berries. Simmer, stirring and mashing the berries, until mixture is thick and clear. Remove from heat and stir in lemon juice, peel, and remaining blueberries. Cool slightly, then fill shell and chill pie. Serve with sweetened whipped cream.

Fruit Pie

Canned apricots, peaches, or pears   1 quart, well drained
Pie shell   9-inch, unbaked
Lemon juice   2 teaspoons (if using commercially canned fruit in heavy syrup)
Crumbly Dutch Topping Mix (see Index)   1 to 1½ cups
Ice cream   topping

Spread fruit in unbaked crust, sprinkle with lemon juice, and spread topping over all. Cover crust edges with foil and bake 35 minutes at 400°. Serve slightly warm with ice cream.
Note: This is best when warm, since the topping does not stay crisp overnight, but it can be recrisped carefully under the broiler.

Pineapple Cheesecake

Crushed pineapple in juice   1 15½-ounce can, well drained
Neufchâtel cheese   1 8-ounce package, softened
Standard Piecrust Mix (see Index)   1 9-inch pie shell, unbaked
Cornstarch   3 tablespoons
Brown sugar   ⅓ cup
Salt   a pinch
Walnuts   ⅓ cup chopped
Crumbly Dutch Topping Mix (see Index)   ½ cup

Beat ½ cup of pineapple into cream cheese; spread mixture in bottom of pie shell. Mix cornstarch, brown sugar, and salt into remaining pineapple, and spread over cream cheese layer. Mix nuts into Crumbly Dutch Topping Mix; spread over pineapple layer. Cover edges of piecrust with foil strips to prevent overbrowning. Bake in bottom ⅓ of oven at 375° for 35 to 40 minutes. Cool before serving.

No-Egg Cheesecake

This is an easy no-bake cheesecake that tastes as good as a baked one.

Bran Crust or graham cracker crust   for 8 by 8-inch pan, plus garnish
Cold water   ¾ cup
Cornstarch Pudding Mix (see Index)   1¼ cups
Pineapple juice   1 cup, hot
Cream cheese or Neufchâtel cheese   1 8-ounce package, cubed and at
    room temperature
Crushed pineapple   garnish, drained (optional)

Prepare Bran Crust. In saucepan, mix cold water with Cornstarch Pudding Mix; stir in hot pineapple juice. Heat to boiling and boil 3 minutes. Add cream cheese and beat with electric mixer until smooth; cool slightly. Pour over crust and sprinkle with reserved crumbs. Chill slightly, garnish with crushed pineapple, and chill several hours. Cut into squares and serve. Serves 6 generously.

Bran Crust

Plain bran flakes (not cereal)   ½ cup
Whole wheat flour   ¼ cup
Sugar   2 tablespoons
Cinnamon   1 teaspoon
Walnuts   ¼ cup finely chopped
Margarine   ¼ cup, melted

Mix all ingredients together. Press ⅔ of mixture into bottom of 8 by 8-inch pan, reserving remainder for garnish.

Mrs. Teed's Special Bran Pineapple Ring

When we go on winery tours, we have a potluck breakfast on the ferry while coming into town. I bring along the Bran Pineapple Ring—hot out of the oven!

Margarine ¼ cup
Sugar ½ cup, or to taste
Pineapple juice ½ cup
All-bran cereal 1 cup
Pineapple juice ⅔ cup
Egg 1
Margarine ¼ cup, softened
Flour 1 cup unsifted
Baking powder 2 teaspoons
Baking soda ½ teaspoon
Salt ½ teaspoon
Sugar ¼ cup

Combine margarine, sugar, and ½ cup pineapple juice; boil 2 minutes. Cool slightly and pour into bottom of greased 8½- or 9-inch ring pan. Combine cereal with ⅔ cup pineapple juice, then beat egg and softened margarine into it. Combine remaining ingredients; add to cereal mixture. Spread carefully over pineapple glaze in pan and bake at 375° for 25 minutes, or until done. Turn upside down on warmed plate and let stand a few minutes, then remove pan, scraping any remaining glaze onto ring. Serve warm. Good for breakfast or brunch, or serve with coffee for dessert.

Quick Blackberry Cake

Flour   1½ cups unsifted
Sugar   ½ cup
Baking powder   2 teaspoons
Salt   a pinch
Egg   1
Milk   ¾ cup
Vanilla   ½ teaspoon
Cooking oil   2 tablespoons
Fresh blackberries   1 cup or
      Frozen blackberries   1 cup, thawed and well drained
Sugar   ⅔ cup
Whipped cream or ice cream   topping

Mix together dry ingredients; add egg, milk, vanilla, and oil; mix well. Spread in greased and floured 8 by 8-inch baking pan. Cover with blackberries and sprinkle with sugar. Bake at 375° for 25 minutes, or until done. Serve warm or cooled with whipped cream.
Variation: Use the Plain Cake Mix (see Index) to make this even quicker.

Almond Cake

I had friends who went to Spain, and they were very impressed with the almond cake. So I said, "We'll make ourselves a plain cake, put sliced almonds on top, pour almond syrup over it, and see if that tastes like Spain." And it did!

Milk   ¾ cup, lukewarm
Plain Cake Mix (see Index)   3⅓ cups
Almond extract   ½ teaspoon
Eggs   2
Sliced almonds   to cover cake
Almond Syrup
Make-Ahead Whipped Cream (see Index)   for frosting (optional) or
   Sweetened whipped cream   for topping (optional)

Add ½ the milk to mix and beat; add remaining milk. Add almond extract and eggs; beat 3 or 4 minutes, then pour into 10-inch springform pan. Bake at 350° for 25 to 30 minutes, or until done. After removing from oven, cover top with almonds and very slowly pour hot Almond Syrup over all. Broil cake until top is bubbly and almonds are lightly browned. Watch carefully to prevent scorching. Cool on rack. This moist cake is very showy, and is good with Make-Ahead Whipped Cream frosting the edges or with whipped cream served on top of each slice.

Almond Syrup

Water   6 tablespoons
Sugar   ¾ cup
Almond extract   ½ teaspoon

Combine sugar and water; boil until it reaches 220°. Remove from heat and add almond extract.

Rum Cake

Milk   ¾ cup, lukewarm
Plain Cake Mix (see Index)   3⅓ cups
Rum flavoring   1 teaspoon
Eggs   2
Coffee Rum Syrup
Make-Ahead Whipped Cream (see Index)   to frost cake

Add ½ the milk to mix and beat; add remaining milk. Add rum flavoring
and eggs; beat 3 to 4 minutes, then pour into 10-inch springform pan.
Bake at 350° for 25 to 30 minutes, or until done. After removing from
oven, spoon hot Coffee Rum Syrup over cake very slowly. When cake is
cool, remove from pan. Frost edges of cake with Make-Ahead Whipped
Cream and decorate top edge of cake.
Variation: Whip instant coffee into the whipped cream.

Coffee Rum Syrup

Strong coffee   ⅓ cup
Sugar   ¾ cup
Rum flavoring   ½ teaspoon
Rum   ¼ cup

Boil coffee and sugar together for 3 minutes. Remove from heat and stir in
rum flavoring and rum.

Oatmeal Cake with Dates and Nuts

Rolled oats* 1 cup
Margarine ½ cup, sliced
Sugar ¾ cup
Brown sugar ¾ cup
Boiling water 1½ cups
Eggs 2
Unbleached flour 1½ cups
Baking soda 1¼ teaspoons
Baking powder ½ teaspoon
Cinnamon 1 teaspoon
Nutmeg ¼ teaspoon
Dates 1 cup sliced
Nuts 1 cup chopped
Topping

Combine oats, margarine, and sugars in large bowl. Add boiling water and set aside 25 minutes. Add next 6 ingredients and beat. Add dates and nuts; mix well. Bake in greased and floured 9 by 13-inch pan at 325° for 40 minutes, or until done. Spread hot topping on hot baked cake and broil just until topping is bubbly. Be careful not to scorch topping.
* Do not use instant rolled oats.

Topping

Margarine ¼ cup
Milk 2 tablespoons
Brown sugar ¾ cup
Nuts ½ cup chopped
Shredded coconut 1 cup

Boil together margarine, milk, and brown sugar for 2 minutes. Remove from heat and stir in nuts and coconut.

Low-Sugar Cake Filling

This is my husband's favorite cake filling. It's not too sweet, and it even freezes well.

Flour   2 tablespoons
Sugar   ½ cup
Milk or skim milk   ½ cup
Margarine   2 tablespoons
Vanilla   1 teaspoon

Combine flour and sugar in small saucepan. Slowly stir in milk, add margarine, and cook over medium heat until thickened, stirring constantly. Remove from heat and stir in vanilla. Cool before using as filling for layer cake.
Variations: Substitute other flavorings for vanilla; add chopped nuts or sweetened shredded coconut.

Blackberry Soda

Sweetened blackberry juice   ⅓ cup
Vanilla ice cream   1 scoop
Soda water

Place blackberry juice in soda glass, add ice cream, and fill with soda water. Makes 1 soda.

Quick Milk Shake

This is fast, easy, and low in calories. On a hot summer day you can have milk shakes on five minutes' notice, and not the fattening ones with ice cream and a lot of artificial ingredients.

Cold water   ¼ cup
Honey or sugar   2 tablespoons
Powdered milk   ¾ cup
Flavoring
Ice cubes   5 to 7, crushed

Put first 4 ingredients in blender; whirl until well blended. Add crushed ice cubes, 1 at a time, and blend at high speed until shake is thick; work quickly for a really thick shake. Serve at once. Makes 2 milk shakes.

Flavorings

Vanilla: Add 1 teaspoon vanilla extract.
Butterscotch: Add 1 teaspoon butterscotch flavoring.
Pineapple: Add 1 teaspoon pineapple extract. To make a real pineapple
   flavored shake, add ½ of a 6-ounce can of frozen concentrated
   pineapple juice, delete cold water, and reduce sweetening.
Chocolate: Add 2 teaspoons chocolate flavoring extract, or add ¼ cup
   chocolate syrup and reduce water and sweetening.
Peach: Add 1 very ripe peach and use only ½ the cold water called for.
Banana: Add 1 very ripe banana and slightly reduce cold water and
   sweetening.
Malted milk: Add 2 teaspoons natural flavor malted milk to any above
   flavoring.
Strawberry: Add ½ cup fresh or frozen strawberries and use only 1
   tablespoon cold water.
Blackberry: Add ½ cup blackberry juice and omit cold water.

Candied Walnuts

We take these along as goodies for the opera.

Evaporated milk   ½ cup
Sugar   1 cup
Cinnamon   1 teaspoon, or to taste
Vanilla   ½ teaspoon
Walnuts   4 cups

Boil together milk, sugar, and cinnamon until mixture reaches 230° on candy thermometer, or until a small thread forms when a little mixture is dropped in cold water. Remove from heat and stir in vanilla and nuts, mixing well. Turn onto waxed paper and separate nuts with a fork. Cool before serving or storing.

Spiced Walnuts

When you make a custard and have egg whites left over, it's always nice to have a few little tricks up your sleeve—something you can do with an egg white, for instance. Instead of making meringue, you can use one egg white this way.

Egg white   1, slightly beaten
Walnuts   4 cups
Sugar   ¼ cup, or to taste
Cinnamon   1 tablespoon

In large bowl, mix egg white and walnuts; stir until nuts are well coated. Combine sugar and cinnamon; mix with nuts. Spread on large cookie sheet and bake at 300° for 30 minutes. Stir with fork to separate nuts, and cool before serving or storing.

Apples

In the country, a lot of apples go to waste. People just let them stay on the ground because they think they are cooking apples and they want eating apples, or vice versa. I'm not such a purist. For one thing, it's practical to find ways of using apples, because they are often free. They also store better than most other fruits. You can have them almost year round. If you wrap them one by one in newspaper and store them in a single layer so they don't touch each other, they'll keep for months.

Apple Leather

Apples
Honey or sugar　to taste
Cinnamon　to taste (optional)
Coconut or flax seed meal*　for fiber (optional)

Puree raw or cooked apples in blender; add remaining ingredients. Spread plastic wrap on screen shelf of food dryer, and cover with apple mixture to ¼-inch thickness. Dry 1 or 2 days, or until mixture is dry and leathery; time depends on type of dryer and moisture in apples. When apple leather is dry, it can easily be removed from plastic wrap. You may dry it a bit longer on screen shelf. Roll the leather while it is still slightly warm, and it will roll without cracking. Cool completely, then wrap and store. Apple leather will keep about 1 month at room temperature, 6 months in a plastic bag in the refrigerator, or for over a year if well wrapped and stored in freezer.
* This will help thicken the leather.
Note:　If you don't have a food dryer, pour thin layer of apple mixture over plastic wrap on cookie sheet. Set oven at lowest setting and dry apple mixture overnight, leaving oven door slightly ajar.

Deluxe Applesauce

This applesauce is made without sugar. The secret is using apple juice instead of water.

Yellow transparent apples or other sweet juicy apples
　　4 cups peeled and sliced
Frozen concentrated apple juice　½ cup thawed
Margarine　1 tablespoon
Cinnamon　a pinch
Vanilla　¼ teaspoon

Slowly cook apples in apple juice and margarine, stirring often to prevent sticking. When very tender, add cinnamon and vanilla; mash gently with fork until smooth. This may be served with cream for breakfast, or over vanilla ice cream for dessert. Sprinkle with additional cinnamon, if desired. Serves 4.
Note:　For baking, you can usually use 1½ cups of unsweetened applesauce to replace 1 cup liquid and ¼ cup sugar.

Apple Pancakes

Egg 1, lightly beaten
Milk ½ cup
Flour ½ cup unsifted
Salt a pinch
Sugar 4 teaspoons
Cornmeal 2 tablespoons
Cinnamon 1 teaspoon
Nutmeg ½ teaspoon
Baking powder 2 teaspoons
Apple 1, peeled and thinly sliced
Margarine 1 tablespoon, melted
Syrup, sour cream, and/or whipped butter topping

Combine egg and milk; mix in next 7 ingredients. Add apple slices and margarine; mix well. Spoon batter onto hot greased griddle and bake on each side. Serve with syrup. Serves 2 to 3.
Variation: This is even faster if you use the Pancake Mix (see Index), adding the apple and spices to the batter.

Special Crusty Baked Apples

Flour ⅓ cup
Sugar ⅔ cup
Cinnamon ½ teaspoon
Nutmeg ¼ teaspoon
Margarine ⅓ cup
Large baking apples 4 to 6, peeled and cored
Egg 1, beaten
Frozen concentrated orange juice ½ cup
Water ¼ cup

Mix together flour, sugar, and spices; cut in margarine with pastry blender. Roll apples in egg, then in crumbly mixture. Arrange in oiled baking pan and fill the centers with any leftover crumbly mix. Dilute orange juice with water and pour around apples. Bake at 350° for 45 to 55 minutes, or until apples are barely tender. Serve warm with orange sauce from pan, which will be quite thick. Good with whipped cream or ice cream. Serves 4 to 6.

Apple Tapioca

Tapioca   ⅓ cup
Light brown sugar   1 cup or less
Apples   3 to 4 cups peeled and thinly sliced
Lemon juice   2 tablespoons
Margarine   2 tablespoons
Salt   ¼ teaspoon
Cinnamon   ½ teaspoon or more
Water   2 cups
Ice cream   topping
Cinnamon or nutmeg   garnish

Combine first 8 ingredients in saucepan; set aside 5 minutes, then slowly bring to a boil, stirring constantly. Cook about 10 minutes, or until apples are tender. Serve warm with ice cream and sprinkle with cinnamon. Serves 4 to 6.
Note: If you're in a hurry, soak tapioca, sugar, lemon juice, margarine, salt, and cinnamon in 1 cup water for 5 minutes. Meanwhile, cook apples in 1 cup water for 5 minutes. Add tapioca mixture to apples and cook 5 minutes more, stirring constantly.

Sugarless Applesauce Dessert

Cottage cheese   8 ounces
Crushed pineapple in juice   ¼ cup, juice drained and reserved
Celery   ¼ cup chopped
Nuts   ½ cup chopped
Mayonnaise   1 tablespoon
Unflavored gelatin   1 tablespoon
Reserved pineapple juice   ½ cup
Unsweetened applesauce   1½ cups or
    Sweetened applesauce   1½ cups and
    Lemon juice   ½ teaspoon
Dietetic whipped topping or sweetened whipped cream   topping

Whip cottage cheese in blender until smooth, then mix in pineapple, celery, nuts, and mayonnaise; set aside. Soften gelatin in pineapple juice, heating over low heat to dissolve completely. Stir into applesauce, mixing well. Pour ½ of gelatin mixture into 8 by 8-inch pan or into individual parfait glasses. Chill until thick but not set. Cover with cottage cheese mixture, then top with remaining gelatin mixture. Chill until set. Top with dietetic whipped topping.

Apple Bar Cookies

Flour ½ cup unsifted
Baking powder 1¼ teaspoons
Salt ½ teaspoon
Sugar ⅔ to ¾ cup
Vanilla 1 teaspoon
Egg 1
Oil 1 to 2 tablespoons (optional)
Apples 1 cup peeled and finely diced
Nuts ½ cup chopped

Mix together dry ingredients. Mix in vanilla, egg, oil, and apples; batter will be very thick. Stir in nuts. Spread batter in greased 8 by 8-inch baking pan. Bake at 350° for about 25 minutes. Cool and cut into bars. **Note:** If you make a double recipe of this, bake it in two 8 by 8-inch pans; do not bake in one large pan or the center will not bake well.

Date-Applesauce-Oatmeal Bars

Margarine ¾ cup
Brown sugar 1 cup
Sugar ½ cup
Egg 1
Flour 2 cups unsifted
Baking soda 1 teaspoon
Salt ½ teaspoon
Nutmeg ½ teaspoon
Applesauce ¾ cup
Dates 1 cup chopped
Rolled oats 2 cups
Ice cream topping

Beat together margarine, sugars, and egg until light and fluffy. Stir flour, baking soda, salt, and nutmeg together and add to sugar mixture along with applesauce; batter will be thick. Stir in oats and dates. Spread in greased 10 by 15 by 2-inch baking pan or in 9 by 13-inch pan plus a small pan. Bake at 350° for 25 to 30 minutes, or until done. Cool in pan, then cut into squares. Serve warm with ice cream for dessert, then cool and use as bar cookie.

Apple Dumplings

Pastry   enough for 9-inch double-crust pie
Apples   3, peeled and sliced
Sugar   ½ cup
Cinnamon   1 teaspoon
Salt   a pinch
Margarine   2 tablespoons, melted
Cream, cinnamon sauce, or ice cream   topping

Roll out pastry and cut into 5-inch squares. Toss remaining ingredients together. Put 2 to 3 tablespoons of filling in the middle of each square, fold pastry over filling, and prick tops. Bake at 425° for 30 minutes. Serve with cream. Makes 6 dumplings.
Variation: Pour cinnamon sauce around dumplings in pan for last 10 minutes of baking.

Apple Turnovers

Apples   6 cups peeled and sliced
Apple juice   ½ cup
Sugar   ½ cup
Cinnamon   1 teaspoon
Nutmeg   ⅛ teaspoon
Cornstarch   2 tablespoons
Cold water   2 tablespoons
Lemon juice   1 tablespoon
Margarine   1 tablespoon
Pastry   enough for 5 piecrusts

Cook together first 5 ingredients until apples are barely tender. Dissolve cornstarch in cold water, and add to apples along with lemon juice; stir mixture gently until thickened. Add margarine, stirring it in as it melts. Set aside to cool. Roll out pastry and cut into 4-inch rounds; a circular metal hamburger press works well. Put a spoonful of apple filling in the center of each round. Moisten the edges, fold them over, and press edges together to seal. Place on cookie sheets and bake 15 to 18 minutes at 350°. Cool on racks. Makes about 2 dozen turnovers.
Note: If served with ice cream, these need no frosting. Otherwise, they will look festive if you make a thin powdered sugar glaze and dribble it over them.

Sugarless Applesauce Pielets*

These tarts require no baking; you can prepare them in no time before supper and they'll be ready in time for dessert. If you use dietetic applesauce, leave out the liquid sweetener, as this applesauce usually has a nonsugar sweetener already in it.

Graham cracker   1
Cinnamon   to taste
Unsweetened applesauce   ½ cup
Liquid artificial sweetener   4 drops or less
Margarine   ½ teaspoon, melted
Vanilla   ¼ teaspoon
Dietetic whipped topping   1 tablespoon (optional)

Crush the graham cracker into an oiled individual serving size pie tin; spread crumbs evenly over bottom of tin and dust with cinnamon. Mix next 4 ingredients together and carefully spoon over graham cracker crumbs. Dust with more cinnamon and set aside for about 30 minutes to allow moisture from applesauce to soak into the crumbs. Top with dietetic whipped topping. Makes 1 pielet.
Note: This recipe was originally designed for diabetics. In the diabetic Exchange System, 1 pielet = 1 serving fruit, ⅓ serving bread, and ½ fat exchange.
* Published in the Seattle *Post-Intelligencer* as "My Favorite Recipe."

Fast Apple Cobbler

Canned Apple Slices, Unthickened (see Index)   1 quart
Cornstarch
Crumbly Dutch Topping Mix (see Index)   1½ cups

Drain juice from apple slices; measure, then pour into saucepan. Add 1 tablespoon cornstarch per ½ cup juice and heat, stirring constantly, until thickened. Arrange apple slices in 8 by 8-inch pan, cover with thickened juice, and top with Crumbly Dutch Topping Mix. Bake at 400° for 20 to 30 minutes, or until topping is lightly browned.
Variation: For extra richness, stir 1 tablespoon butter or margarine into thickened juice.

Candied Apple Crisp

The topping is almost the same as the Crumbly Dutch Topping Mix, except this one is made with brown sugar.

Fine whole wheat flour   1 cup unsifted
Brown sugar   1 cup
Cinnamon   ½ teaspoon
Nutmeg   ⅛ teaspoon
Salt   ⅛ teaspoon
Margarine   ½ cup
Apples   4 to 6 cups sliced

Mix flour, sugar, spices, and salt, making sure there are no lumps in brown sugar. Cut in margarine with pastry blender until mixture is in fine crumbs. Arrange the apples in large oiled casserole or in individual serving dishes or tart pans. Pat the topping mixture onto the apples and bake at 350°, 35 to 40 minutes for casserole, 20 to 25 minutes for individual dishes. The topping fuses together and gets really crunchy, so do not overbrown. Serve warm. Makes enough topping to cover 1 large casserole or 8 individual dishes.
Note: This recipe should not be made more than an hour before serving, since the topping does not remain crisp. Other fruits, such as canned pears or peaches, can be substituted for the apples. Drain the fruit, and bake only long enough to brown topping nicely.

Quick Apple Pie

Canned Apple Slices, Thickened (see Index)   1 quart
Pie shell   baked
Whipping cream   ½ pint, whipped and sweetened

Warm the apple filling until the jelled part is semi-liquid. Remove the apple slices with a slotted spoon and layer them in pie shell. Pour the warmed juice over the apples and chill pie in refrigerator until cold and set. Frost with whipped cream before serving.

Apple Batter Pie

This is a crustless pie.

Large apples   3, sliced
Cinnamon   ¾ teaspoon
Sugar   ⅓ cup
Walnuts   ½ cup chopped
Flour   1 cup unsifted
Sugar   ¾ cup
Margarine   ½ cup, melted and cooled
Eggs   2, beaten
Ice cream   topping

Arrange apples in oiled 9-inch pie tin. Sprinkle with cinnamon and sugar, then with walnuts. Mix together remaining ingredients and pour over apples. Do not fill too full, or the batter will run over. Bake at 300° for 30 minutes, or until batter is firm. Serve in wedges with ice cream.

Grated Apple Pie

This is another crustless pie.

Sugar   ¾ cup
Egg   1
Flour   5 tablespoons
Salt   a pinch
Baking powder   1½ teaspoons
Vanilla   1 teaspoon
Apples   1 cup peeled and grated
Nuts   ½ cup chopped

Cream together sugar and egg, then stir in dry ingredients and vanilla. Fold in apple and nuts, and pour into buttered 9-inch pie tin. Do not fill pie tin too full, as mixture rises while baking and may run over. Bake at 350° for 40 to 45 minutes. Serve in wedges while still slightly warm. Good with ice cream.

Apple Butter Pie

Very thick apple butter   1⅓ cups or
   Thick applesauce   1⅓ cups, extra spices added
Eggs   2, beaten
Evaporated milk   1⅓ cups (less if apple butter is thin)
Brown sugar   ½ cup
Cinnamon   1 teaspoon
Salt   a pinch
Pie shell   8-inch, unbaked
Ice cream or whipped cream   topping

Combine first 6 ingredients and pour into pie shell. Protect crust edges with ribbon of foil to prevent overbrowning. Bake 15 minutes at 425°, then lower heat to 350° and bake 40 to 45 minutes, or until knife inserted in center comes out clean. Serve hot or cool, with ice cream.

Apple Pie

Instant tapioca   ¼ cup
Cinnamon   1 teaspoon
Canned Apple Slices, Unthickened (see Index)   1 quart
Double-crust pie shell   unbaked
Margarine   to taste

Add tapioca and cinnamon to apple slices. Turn into pie shell, dot with margarine, and cover with top crust. Cut slits in crust and cover edges with foil to prevent overbrowning. Bake at 425° for 15 minutes, then lower heat to 350° and bake 30 minutes more, or until done.

Betty's Apple Pie

Water or concentrated apple juice   ½ cup
Cornstarch   2 tablespoons
Sugar   ¾ cup (slightly less if using apple juice)
Cinnamon   ½ teaspoon
Margarine   1 tablespoon
Double-crust pie shell   unbaked
Apples   4 cups peeled and sliced

In saucepan, mix together water and cornstarch. Bring to a boil, add sugar, and simmer until thick; add cinnamon and margarine, and set aside. Bake bottom crust 5 minutes at 400°. Fill with sliced apples and pour cornstarch mixture over apples. Cover with top crust; cut slits in crust and cover edges with strip of foil to prevent overbrowning. Bake at 350° for 35 minutes, or until top is brown and apples are done.

Apple Kuchen*

There's only ½ cup of sugar in the whole recipe!

Flour   1½ cups unsifted
Salt   ¼ teaspoon
Baking powder   2 teaspoons
Baking soda   ¼ teaspoon
Margarine   ¼ cup
Egg   1
Milk   ⅓ cup
Apples   4 to 5, peeled and sliced
Topping

Mix dry ingredients; cut in margarine until crumbly. Beat egg into milk, add to flour mixture, and stir. Dough will be very stiff. Pat evenly over the bottom of a 9 by 13-inch pan. Place apple slices in overlapping rows on top of dough. Bake at 400° for about 25 minutes, remove from oven, and spread topping on evenly. Lower heat to 350° and bake 15 to 20 minutes more, or until golden. Best when served warm.
Variation: Substitute fresh peaches for apples.
* This recipe was originally published in the *Bainbridge Arts and Crafts Starving Artists Cook Book,* published by Bainbridge Arts and Crafts, Inc.

Topping

Margarine   ¼ cup, softened
Sugar   ½ cup
Nutmeg   ¼ teaspoon
Cinnamon   ½ teaspoon

Cream together margarine and sugar; stir in spices.

Apple-Filled Cake à la Mode

Rolled oats 1 cup
Flour ⅔ cup unsifted
Sugar ¼ cup
Brown sugar ¼ cup
Nutmeg ¼ teaspoon
Allspice ¼ teaspoon
Margarine ½ cup
Walnuts ⅓ cup chopped
Canned Apple Slices, Thickened (see Index) 1 pint
Ice cream topping
Cinnamon to taste

Combine first 6 ingredients. Cut in margarine, using pastry blender or mixer on low speed, until mixture is crumbly. Mix in nuts. Press ½ of crumbly mixture into an 8 by 8- or 9 by 9-inch pan. Top with apple filling. Spread remaining crumbly mixture over apples and pat down lightly. Bake at 350° for 30 minutes, or until top is nicely browned and filling starts to bubble up. Top each serving with ice cream and sprinkle with cinnamon.

Fresh Apple Cake

Flour 2 cups unsifted
Sugar 2 cups
Baking soda 2 teaspoons
Cinnamon 1 teaspoon
Nutmeg ¼ teaspoon
Salt ¼ teaspoon
Apples 4 cups peeled and finely diced
Margarine ½ cup, softened
Eggs 2
Nuts 1 cup chopped (optional)
Powdered sugar to sprinkle on top
Ice cream topping

Mix together dry ingredients; add apples, margarine, and eggs. Stir in nuts. Do not overmix; batter will be thick. Spread in greased and floured 9 by 13-inch pan. Bake at 325° for 35 to 45 minutes, or until top springs back when pressed. Sprinkle with powdered sugar and cool in pan. Serve warm with ice cream or cold.

Chocolate Apple Cake

Margarine   1 cup, softened
Sugar   2 cups
Eggs   3
Water   ½ cup
Flour   2½ cups
Baking soda   1 teaspoon
Baking powder   ½ teaspoon
Cinnamon   1 teaspoon
Allspice   1 teaspoon
Cocoa   2 tablespoons
Vanilla   1 tablespoon
Chocolate chips   ½ cup
Apple   2 cups grated (peeled or unpeeled)
Nuts   1 cup chopped

Beat together margarine, sugar, and eggs. Add next 8 ingredients; mix thoroughly. Fold in remaining ingredients and pour batter into greased and floured 10-inch tube pan or into 9 by 13-inch baking pan. Bake at 325° for 1 hour, or until done.

Homemade Beer, Wines, and Liqueurs

We began making our own wine when we moved to the country—we had an abundance of fruits and berries, but a dire lack of money. Later on, we began making our own beer and liqueurs, and it's been worth it. Even at inflated 1979 prices, our beer costs only five cents per stubbie, and we like it better than store-bought beer.

If you don't have a local wine supply shop, wine- and beer-making supplies are available through E. C. Kraus, P.O. Box 451, Nevada, Missouri 64772.

Homemade Beer

It will go down in history: 1978 was the year it became legal to make your own beer! To get yourself started, you'll need a ten-gallon plastic fermenting container; a beer hydrometer; eight dozen clean (empty) stubbie beer bottles, the returnable nonscrew-top kind; one gross of bottle caps; and a bottle capper.

Cold water   2 gallons, plus more as needed
Blue Ribbon Malt Extract*   1 3-pound can
Boiling water   ½ gallon
Sugar   4 pounds
Boiling water   ½ gallon
Beer settler   1 packet
Beer yeast   1½ packets
Lukewarm water   ½ cup

Pour cold water into plastic fermenting container. Dissolve malt extract in boiling water, then add to cold water. Dissolve sugar in boiling water and add to container. Stir in beer settler, then add enough cold water to make 8 gallons total liquid. (This must be lukewarm before you add the yeast.) Dissolve yeast in ½ cup lukewarm water; allow to soak 5 minutes. Stir yeast, and add to malt mixture. Float beer hydrometer in liquid, cover top of container with tea towel or other cotton cloth, and fasten it down securely. Place container in warm spot (about 65° is good), and allow to ferment 3 to 5 days. Check hydrometer twice a day; when it sinks to the point where the hydrometer's red line is level with the surface of the beer, it is time to bottle. Fill bottles to within 1½ inches of top; some bottles have a ridge there. Cap them and store beer in cool place for 3 weeks to age. Chill beer well before opening. When pouring into glass, pour slowly to leave sediment in bottle. Rinse out bottles after use and store upside down until needed for next batch of beer.
* You can use Very Pale malt extract, if you like a light beer.
Note: If you are going to make ½ a batch, use 1 packet of beer yeast. Do not transport this beer to picnics. It all will foam right out of the bottle once it gets warm and/or jostled.

Windfall Apple-Rosé Wine

Campden tablets 4
Water 3 gallons
Apples 25 pounds, cored, chopped, and bruises removed
Sugar 10 pounds
Boiling water 3 quarts
Yeast nutrient 1¼ teaspoons
All-purpose dry wine yeast 1 package
Pectic enzyme 1¼ teaspoons
Lukewarm water 1½ cups, plus more as needed
Sugar ½ pound
Frozen concentrated grape juice 1 16-ounce can, boiling
Cold water as needed

In bucket or container, dissolve tablets in water; add apples, cover, and soak overnight. The next day, dissolve sugar in boiling water and add to apples. Dissolve nutrient, yeast, and enzyme in ½ cup lukewarm water each. When apple mixture is lukewarm, add dissolved nutrient, yeast, and enzyme. Keep container covered and stir morning and evening for 5 days, then strain or press apple juice into 5-gallon carboy. Dissolve remaining ½ pound of sugar in boiling grape juice, add enough cold water to cool it to lukewarm, then add to apple liquid in carboy. Add enough more lukewarm water to fill carboy almost to neck, fit with water seal, and put in warm place between 65° and 70°. After 7 days, add enough more lukewarm water to fill up to top of neck, about 2 inches from water seal. When wine has completed fermentation (no bubbles at all around the top and no tiny bubbles coming up), carefully siphon the wine off the sediment into a clean 5-gallon carboy. Put it in a cool place to clear before final bottling. Makes 5 gallons.

Blackberry Juice Wine

The steam juicer has quite revolutionized winemaking at our house. We no longer have to ferment it all during fresh fruit season, which is also our busiest time of year with the vegetable garden, as well as busiest time with spinning yarn for our one big craft fair sale. Formerly, the only alternative was to put the berries and fruit in the freezer, but there wasn't enough freezer space to take care of it all. Now we bottle quarts of blackberry juice and make wine in the winter out of that and any other berries and fruits that are available free or reasonably priced.

Blackberry juice*   3 quarts
Sugar   8 pounds
Boiling water   ½ gallon
Cool water   as needed
Wine nutrient or yeast energizer   1½ teaspoons
Lukewarm water   1½ cups, plus more as needed
Pectic enzyme   1 teaspoon
All-purpose dry wine yeast   1 package
Sugar   2 pounds
Boiling water   1 quart
Cold water or berry wine   as needed

Empty blackberry juice into 5 gallon food-grade (polyethylene) plastic fermentation container. In large kettle, dissolve sugar in boiling water and add to blackberry juice. Add enough cool water to bring juice mixture to 4 gallons; temperature should be lukewarm. Dissolve nutrient in ½ cup lukewarm water; add to juice. Dissolve pectic enzyme in ½ cup lukewarm water; add to juice. Soften wine yeast in remaining ½ cup lukewarm water for 10 minutes, mix to dissolve, and add to juice. Mix well. Cover top of container with clean tea towel or cotton cloth, and fasten down securely. (The elastic from the top of an old pair of pantyhose is perfect for fastening the cloth around the top.) Put the container in a warm place, about 65° to 70°. Stir it morning and night for 5 days, then pour it all into a 5-gallon carboy fitted with a water seal (fermentation lock) and place the carboy in the same warm spot. After several days, dissolve the remaining 2 pounds of sugar in 1 quart boiling water; cool it to lukewarm and pour into carboy. After a few more days, fill the carboy to within 3 inches of the bottom of the water seal with lukewarm water. Leave it to ferment completely. Evidence of fermentation will be tiny bubbles rising to form a bead of bubbles at the top of the wine, as well as bubbles through the water seal, which slow down and may seem to have stopped. When these have ceased completely, the wine is done fermenting. Now, siphon it off into a clean carboy, being careful not to disturb the sediment on the bottom. If the carboy is not sitting high enough for siphoning, move it onto a chair or table and wait 24 hours before siphoning so sediment can resettle. Add enough cold water to fill carboy to within 2 inches of bottom of water seal. Place carboy in a cool place to clear. (With wine made from steamed juice, you will be pleasantly surprised at how fast it clears, usually within a month.) You may re-siphon the wine off the small amount of sediment into another clean carboy and leave it to age a few months, or you may siphon it into bottles to enjoy now. Always store homemade wine in a cool place after it is bottled, to avoid refermentation. Unless it is filtered or treated with Sorbistat K or some similar chemical, there is always some chance of refermentation, which could break the bottles. Makes 5 gallons.

* Use only juice made in steam canner (see Index).

Variations: This makes a fairly dry wine; for a sweeter wine you could use a little more sugar—1 pound more for a medium dry wine, 2 to 3 pounds more for a sweet wine. Actually, the sweetness of the berries themselves can vary due to location and the stage of ripeness, but 10 pounds of sugar is a fair average to use if you want fairly dry wine. We use the same quantity of sugar for Apple Juice Wine, also made with 3 quarts of steamed juice to yield 5 gallons of wine. For Rhubarb Juice Wine, we like the acid content best when we use only 2 quarts of rhubarb juice for 5 gallons of wine and increase the sugar to 11 pounds total. Pear Juice Wine is also very successful.

Homemade Orange Liqueur

Most homemade liqueurs require expensive, special flavorings or extracts that make only one fifth of liqueur. My recipes use only what you might have on the shelf or in the fridge.

Sugar   1 cup
Light corn syrup   1 cup
Orange peel   of 2 oranges, in ½-inch wide strips
Fresh orange juice   3 cups
Vodka   1½ cups

In heavy 2-quart saucepan, melt sugar over low heat for 5 minutes, or until melted and amber-colored. Remove from heat and slowly pour in corn syrup, stirring until blended. Add orange peel and orange juice. Bring mixture to a boil, cover, and simmer 10 minutes. Remove from heat, cool, and add vodka. Pour into tightly covered container; store 2 weeks at room temperature to blend flavors, then strain into sterilized glass container and refrigerate. Makes 3 pints.

Homemade Coffee Liqueur

This will keep indefinitely, and it gets smoother as it ages.

Brown sugar   1½ cups
Sugar   ⅔ cup
Water   2 cups
Instant powdered coffee   ½ cup
Vanilla   2 tablespoons
100 proof vodka   3 cups

Add sugars to water and bring to a boil; boil several minutes. Stir coffee in slowly, remove mixture from heat, and cool slightly. Add vanilla and vodka. Bottle liqueur and age at least 2 weeks. Makes about 5 cups.
Note: This is delightful mixed with cream or served over ice cream. You can use it in a cream gelatin or add it to a pudding as you would vanilla—after it's removed from the heat (you don't want to boil away the liquor). If you are using 80 proof vodka, decrease the water slightly.

Homemade Almond Liqueur

Almonds   1 cup chopped
Peach pit kernels   1 cup chopped
Ground coriander   ½ teaspoon
Cinnamon   ⅓ teaspoon
100 proof vodka   2 cups
Sugar   2 cups
Water   1 cup

Add almonds, peach kernels and spices to vodka; set aside for 6 to 9 weeks, then strain through cloth. Boil together sugar and water, then cool and mix with strained vodka. Set aside 2 weeks, then pour liquor off any sediment in the bottom, and bottle. Makes about 1 quart.
Note: If you are using 80 proof vodka, decrease water to ¾ cup. If you wish to increase the almond flavor, add several drops of almond extract.

Homemade Italiano Liqueur

This has a lot of kick to it.

Sugar   2 cups
Water   ⅔ cup
Lime juice   of 1 lime, or 1 tablespoon
Vanilla   1 tablespoon
Anise extract   ½ teaspoon
100 proof vodka   2½ cups

Bring sugar and water to a boil. Remove from heat and add remaining ingredients in order given. Bottle and age at least 2 weeks. Makes well over a fifth of liqueur.
Note: Use 2 tablespoons more vodka and 2 tablespoons less water if vodka is only 80 proof.

Canning

I've always been enthusiastic about canning, so it doesn't seem like work. I usually can enough to last two or three years, especially if I get a really good buy on something. Sometimes, come the next year, I'll miss out on them, so it's good to be prepared. Last year, for instance, I got free pears from a spinning student who just wasn't using them. I went crazy over them; I kept going back and getting more. A few months later, she sold the place, so I won't get any more free pears, but in the meantime I canned enough to last three years.

Canning used to mean a fantastic mess in the kitchen—steamed up windows and dripping jelly bags. But no more. I can't really take credit for the easy system I have now; I just discovered two grand pieces of equipment and I make as much use of them as possible.

The Steam Juicer

The steam juicer I use is stainless steel, so it can be used with all acid fruits and berries, as well as for other purposes, such as steaming vegetables before freezing, steaming clams, or cooking corn on the cob. The cookbooklet that comes with the juicer has detailed instructions for its use and also contains recipes for using the juice and for using the pulp that remains in the fruit basket. (We make fruit leathers from the pulp.) The juice itself can be used to make jelly, wine, or a number of different desserts.

It takes an average of one hour for most fruits or berries to steam. At the end of that time, the juice may be bottled directly from the juice catcher into heated bottles. You need not use your good canning jars, either—you can use pop bottles or quart-size beer bottles. We favor the quart beer bottles, since a quart is a convenient size for all our uses and the amber glass protects the color of the bottled juice. A reusable rubber cap (made in West Germany and sold by the distributor of the juicer) makes the bottling simple, so there's no need to process the bottles in any way to seal them. The juice is bottled by releasing the clamp on the tube from the juice catcher and letting the juice flow into the heated bottle, filling it to overflowing. The rubber cap is slipped over the top of the bottle and it vacuum-seals as the juice cools. Just store the bottled juice on a shelf in a cool, dark place.

One big advantage of the steam juicer is that you no longer have to can your fruit in sugar syrup. It is possible to steam overripe or imperfect fruit, plus the peelings from everything you prepare for canning, and get good, pure fruit juice to use as canning "syrup." (Sugar can always be added to the juice after you open the fruit, especially if it will be used in a fruit pudding or pie.) You won't believe how good fruit is when it's canned in its own juice. And when the fruit is served, any extra juice can be made into a gelatin dessert or used in tapiocas, fruit sodas, et cetera.

You can purchase a stainless steel juicer from Ashdown House, 612 East Pleasant Way, Bountiful, Utah 84010. They also carry the steam canner.

The Steam Canner

I now use a steam canner for canning acid fruits, tomatoes, relishes, and anything else that is usually processed in a water bath. It uses only three pints of water, so it takes much less time to get up to steam than it takes for a water bath canner to get up to boiling. This means canning time is cut considerably, even though the jars are processed in steam for as long as they would be processed in boiling water. This shorter overall processing time saves energy and water, and also destroys the fruit enzymes more quickly, stopping deterioration and saving the natural fresh fruit flavor and texture. Also, with only three pints of water, you never have to lift a heavy pot to get it onto the stove, or empty it out after canning.

Since the canning jars are sitting on a perforated platform over the water, instead of standing in boiling water, they are easy to remove from the canner and you can put in more jars immediately (I always check the water level first, though). The heat under the canner can be adjusted as soon as the steam is really flowing; high heat is not required for the whole canning period—just enough to keep up a small flow of steam. Since there is less chance of the jars breaking, I use mayonnaise jars and I don't have any problems with them at all.

You may follow the instructions for preparing your fruit, tomatoes, and other acid foods that are given in your canning books, but do not fill the bottles fuller than one inch from the top for cold pack, and half an inch from the top for hot pack. Put the canning screw bands on firmly by hand, but not quite as tightly as possible. Use the same timing for steam processing as that given for boiling water bath processing. And remember, the steam canner is *not* a substitute for a pressure canner.

About L. M. Pectin

L. m. pectin is an abbreviation for low methoxyl pectin. It is made from citrus fruit rinds. The only easy way to dissolve it is to add it to very hot water or fruit juice and blend briefly in a blender.

Unlike most pectins, which depend on sugar to jell, l. m. pectin thickens when used with calcium; dicalcium phosphate is the easiest type to use. This means jellies, jams, and desserts made with l. m. pectin can be made with little or no sugar. (Actually, most jellies and jams taste a lot better when there is a high proportion of fruit to sugar.)

Since sugar acts as a preservative as well as a jelling agent, items made with l. m. pectin cannot be put up in jelly glasses with paraffin on top. Instead, you will need to can them as you would can fruit, in jars with two-piece metal lids that seal. They must then be processed in a steam or water bath canner for a short time.

L. m. pectin and dicalcium phosphate can be purchased from Walnut Acres, Penns Creek, Pennsylvania 17862.

Basic Jelly or Jam

Fruit juice   as available or
   Fruit or berries   as available, mashed or pureed
Sugar   ¼ cup per cup of juice or fruit, or to taste or
   Artificial sweetener   to taste
L. m. pectin   ½ teaspoon per cup of juice or fruit
Dicalcium phosphate   ⅛ teaspoon
Water   ¼ cup

Heat juice together with sugar until hot. Pour about ½ cup of very hot juice into blender, cover, and put blender on low. Remove lid, add pectin, and blend on high until pectin is dissolved. Add to remaining juice and mix well. Stir dicalcium phosphate into water; stir well before measuring each teaspoon of solution, as it never really dissolves. Stir dicalcium phosphate solution into juice 1 teaspoon at a time. Chill a dab of jelly in freezer and check for proper thickness. If it is not thick enough, add another teaspoon of solution to jelly and test again. Continue until proper thickness is achieved. Reheat to boiling and pour hot jelly into hot, sterile ½-pint canning jars, leaving ½-inch headspace. Top with lids and screw metal bands on firmly. Make sure lids are sealed, or process in canner for 5 minutes. After opening, keep jelly refrigerated.

Canned Apple Slices, Thickened

This is a low-calorie filling, since it is thickened with pectin instead of cornstarch.

Apples as available
Water 1 quart
Powdered ascorbic acid ¼ teaspoon or
    Commercial ascorbic acid mix according to directions
Canned apple juice 4 cups, sweetened to taste or
    Frozen apple juice 4 cups, diluted and sweetened to taste
L. m. pectin 1 tablespoon
Dicalcium phosphate ⅛ teaspoon
Water 1 tablespoon

Peel and slice apples into water mixed with ascorbic acid, to prevent darkening. Bring apple juice to a boil; pour 2 cups into blender container and put top on blender. Cover blender with folded towel to hold top on. Turn on blender, them remove top and add pectin. Blend quickly, then pour out immediately into saucepan containing the remaining apple juice. Mix dicalcium phosphate with 1 tablespoon water, stir well (it will not dissolve), and add ½ teaspoon of mixture to apple juice. Test for firmness by spooning out 1 tablespoon of apple juice mixture and putting it in the freezer for 1 minute to chill. If it is not thick enough when cooled, add ½ teaspoon more of dicalcium solution and test again. When juice is as thick as desired, place well-drained apple slices in pint or quart jars. Pour boiling apple juice mixture over them, seal, and process jars in canner;* 15 minutes for pints, 20 minutes for quarts.
* Use only steam or water bath canner.

Canned Apple Slices, Unthickened

Apples 8 cups sliced
Sugar 1½ cups
Powdered ascorbic acid 1 teaspoon or
    Commercial ascorbic acid mix 2 teaspoons

Place sliced apples in stainless steel bowl or pan. Combine sugar and ascorbic acid; sprinkle over apples. Toss lightly and let stand several hours to make its own juice. (You can layer several large pans at a time.) Fill pint or quart canning jars with apple slices and juice. Process jars in canner* for 20 minutes. Makes 2 quarts.
* Use only steam or water bath canner.

Apple Chutney

This is a good condiment for people on low-sodium diets, as it contains no salt.

Apples 2 quarts with peels
Onions 3
Large green peppers 2
Raisins ⅔ cup
Cider vinegar 1½ cups
Frozen concentrated orange juice ⅓ cup thawed
Lemon juice 3 tablespoons or
    Lemon juice and rind of 1 to 2 lemons
Celery seed 1 tablespoon
Date crystals* ½ cup or
    Dates ⅔ cup chopped
Honey ¾ cup

Chop apples, onions, peppers, and raisins in blender, a little at a time, using part of vinegar with each to help it chop. Do not blend too finely. Place in saucepan, add remaining ingredients, and simmer until thick. Pour into ½-pint jars, top with heated lids, and process in canner for 10 minutes. Makes 3 to 3½ pints.
* If date crystals are not available in your area, you may purchase them by mail from Shields Date Gardens, 80-225 Highway 111, Indio, California 92201.

Bette Stuart's Dill Pickles

Small pickling cucumbers whole or
    Large pickling cucumbers halved
Fresh heads of dill as needed
Garlic cloves as needed
Horseradish root as needed
Water 2 quarts
Vinegar 1 quart
Pickling salt ⅔ cup
Alum 1 teaspoon

Wash cucumbers with vegetable brush and drain. Rinse dill and garlic. Wash, peel, and slice horseradish into 1-inch slices for ½-gallon jars, ½-inch slices for quart jars. Wash canning jars. In the bottom of each jar place 2 heads of dill, 2 garlic cloves, and 1 slice of horseradish. Pack larger cucumbers in bottom of jars, add another head of dill, then pack smaller cucumbers on top. Boil together water, vinegar, and salt; add alum. Set cucumber-filled jars in sink with 3 inches of very hot water around them. Pour boiling vinegar solution into a jar, to within ½ inch of top. Wipe off top of jar and seal with sterilized lid, which should seal as it cools. Continue canning, doing 1 jar at a time. Make sure lids are sealed, or process jars in canner for 5 minutes. Make more syrup as necessary, until you use up cucumbers. Store pickles 6 weeks before eating.

Pickled Beets

These use no salt and very little sugar.

Vinegar 1 pint
Frozen concentrated apple juice ½ cup thawed
Sugar ¼ cup
Whole cloves 6
Whole allspice 1 teaspoon
Cinnamon sticks 1 to 2
Beets 3 pounds, cooked, skinned, and sliced

Heat together vinegar, apple juice, and sugar. Tie spices in cloth bag, add to vinegar mixture, and boil 1 minute. Remove spices and add sliced beets. Boil 5 minutes, then remove beets with slotted spoon and pack into sterile pint jars. Fill jars with boiling vinegar mixture and seal with sterilized lids, doing 1 jar at a time. Make sure lids are sealed, or process jars in canner for 5 minutes. Makes 3 pints.
Note: When you get down to the last few beets in the jar, you can add gelatin to the beet juice, chop the beets and stir them into the thickened juice, then chill all for a delicious salad. Serve in individual molds, topped with a spoonful of mayonnaise.

Canned Orange-Banana Pudding

I buy bananas only when they are on sale really cheap. Then I overbuy. I slice some with a butter-pat cutter and dry them; others I mash and freeze for banana bread. Then there's this delicious canned dessert.

Sugar   1 to 2 cups
Bananas   5 pounds, mashed to equal 6 cups
Orange juice   1 cup
L. m. pectin   1½ tablespoons
Dicalcium phosphate   ⅛ teaspoon
Water   ¼ cup
Butter or margarine   2 tablespoons, melted (optional)

Add sugar to bananas; heat gently to boiling. In separate pan, bring orange juice to boil. Pour hot juice into blender; add about 1 cup of banana mixture. Put lid on blender and cover it with a towel. Turn blender on low, remove lid, and add pectin all at once; turn blender on high, blend well, then pour into remaining banana mixture. Stir and simmer 1 minute. Stir dicalcium phosphate into water and add 6 teaspoons to banana mixture, stirring dicalcium phosphate solution each time before measuring a teaspoon. Stir pudding, then chill a spoonful several minutes in the freezer to check thickness. If more thickness is desired, add 1 more teaspoon of solution, stir, and test again. When proper thickness is achieved, add butter to pudding and stir well. Pour pudding into hot ½-pint jars, leaving ½-inch headspace. Wipe off rims, top with lids boiled according to directions, and screw metal bands on firmly, but not as tightly as possible. Process 10 minutes in canner. Serve pudding with cream. Makes about 3½ pints.

Canned Pear-Pineapple Dessert

Ripe pears   4 to 6 pounds, peeled and cored
Water   1 quart
Powdered ascorbic acid   ¼ teaspoon or
   Commercial ascorbic acid mix   according to directions
Fresh pineapples   2, peeled, cored, and chunked or
   Pineapple chunks in juice   3 20-ounce cans, juice drained and
     reserved
Unsweetened pineapple juice   1 48-ounce can
L. m. pectin   4 teaspoons, plus as needed
Dicalcium phosphate   ⅛ teaspoon
Water   ¼ cup
Sugar or artificial sweetener   to taste (optional)
Butter or margarine   3 tablespoons (optional)

Cut pears into quarters or chunks and add to water mixed with ascorbic acid. Measure reserved pineapple juice if you're using canned pineapple, then add to canned pineapple juice. Measure out pectin, adding an additional ½ teaspoon for each scant cup of reserved pineapple juice; set aside. Heat juice to boiling, then pour 2 cups into blender. Put lid on blender and hold folded towel over the top before turning blender on. Turn blender on low, remove lid, and add pectin all at once. Blend on high for 1 minute, then pour mixture into remaining hot pineapple juice and stir well. Mix dicalcium phosphate with water; since it does not dissolve, stir well before measuring each teaspoon. Add 1 teaspoon of dicalcium phosphate solution for each cup of hot pineapple juice; stir well. Chill a spoonful of mixture in freezer for several minutes and check for thickness. It should be as stiff as a gelatin dessert. If mixture should be firmer, add another teaspoon of solution and test again. When desired thickness is achieved, adjust for sweetness, add drained pear chunks and pineapple chunks, stir, and heat to simmering. Add butter for extra richness; mix well. Ladle boiling fruit and juice into sterilized jars, leaving ½-inch headspace. Wipe off rims, put on lids that have been boiled according to directions, and screw on metal rings firmly, but not as tightly as possible. Process jars in canner;* 10 minutes for ½-pint jars, 15 minutes for pint jars. Makes about 8 to 10 pints.
* Use only steam or water bath canner.

U.S. and Metric Measurements

Approximate conversion formulas are given below for commonly used U.S. and metric kitchen measurements.

Teaspoons	x	5	= milliliters
Tablespoons	x	15	= milliliters
Fluid ounces	x	30	= milliliters
Fluid ounces	x	0.03	= liters
Cups	x	240	= milliliters
Cups	x	0.24	= liters
Pints	x	0.47	= liters
Dry pints	x	0.55	= liters
Quarts	x	0.95	= liters
Dry quarts	x	1.1	= liters
Gallons	x	3.8	= liters
Ounces	x	28	= grams
Ounces	x	0.028	= kilograms
Pounds	x	454	= grams
Pounds	x	0.45	= kilograms
Milliliters	x	0.2	= teaspoons
Milliliters	x	0.07	= tablespoons
Milliliters	x	0.034	= fluid ounces
Milliliters	x	0.004	= cups
Liters	x	34	= fluid ounces
Liters	x	4.2	= cups
Liters	x	2.1	= pints
Liters	x	1.82	= dry pints
Liters	x	1.06	= quarts
Liters	x	0.91	= dry quarts
Liters	x	0.26	= gallons
Grams	x	0.035	= ounces
Grams	x	0.002	= pounds
Kilograms	x	35	= ounces
Kilograms	x	2.2	= pounds

Temperature Equivalents

Fahrenheit	− 32	× 5	÷ 9	= Celsius
Celsius	× 9	÷ 5	+ 32	= Fahrenheit

U.S. Equivalents

1 teaspoon	= ⅓ tablespoon
1 tablespoon	= 3 teaspoons
2 tablespoons	= 1 fluid ounce
4 tablespoons	= ¼ cup or 2 ounces
5⅓ tablespoons	= ⅓ cup or 2⅔ ounces
8 tablespoons	= ½ cup or 4 ounces
16 tablespoons	= 1 cup or 8 ounces
⅜ cup	= ¼ cup plus 2 tablespoons
⅝ cup	= ½ cup plus 2 tablespoons
⅞ cup	= ¾ cup plus 2 tablespoons
1 cup	= ½ pint or 8 fluid ounces
2 cups	= 1 pint or 16 fluid ounces
1 liquid quart	= 2 pints or 4 cups
1 liquid gallon	= 4 quarts

Metric Equivalents

1 milliliter	= 0.001 liter
1 liter	= 1000 milliliters
1 milligram	= 0.001 gram
1 gram	= 1000 milligrams
1 kilogram	= 1000 grams

Index

Other Books from Pacific Search Press